PARENTING WITH
KINGDOM
PURPOSE

PARENTING WITH
KINGDOM
PURPOSE

KEN HEMPHILL
& RICHARD ROSS

NASHVILLE, TENNESSEE

978-0-8054-3299-2

Published by B&H Publishing Group
Nashville, Tennessee

Dewey Decimal Classification: 306.85
Subject Heading: KINGDOM OF GOD \ FAMILY LIFE \
PARENT AND CHILD

7 8 9 10 11 12   14 13 12 11

Dedicated to the memory of Carl and Ruby Hemphill and Paul Moore and in honor of Daphne Moore—parents who try with Paula and me to serve the King.

Dedicated to my parents, Bryan and Alice Ross—at whose feet I learned what parenting with kingdom purpose looks like.

CONTENTS

PREFACE

WHAT IS MY CHILD'S PURPOSE on planet Earth?

As an adult, what is my purpose here?

Until we understand ultimate purpose we will fail at life.

Even if we succeed at sports or business, if we fail to accomplish that for which the Creator designed us, we will fail at life.

We were created by God in his image that we might have a personal relationship with him. We were redeemed so that we might *advance God's kingdom by his power for his glory!*

There are hundreds of books on parenting. This one is unique. It details how to parent with kingdom purpose. No issue could be more central for families.

It is never too late to begin parenting with a view toward kingdom impact. Nor is it ever too early.

GROUP STUDY

Many church leaders will gather parents to experience this book together. They will find a full teaching plan and other enrichment materials in the book *Transforming Student Ministry: Research Calling for Change* (LifeWay).

APPRECIATION

Special appreciation is extended to Mike Bizzell, Hyojeong Lee, and Heuikwang Shin. These PhD students at Southwestern Baptist Theological Seminary in Fort Worth, Texas, made valuable contributions to the research base of this book. Appreciation also is extended to Cassie Hubbard for her valuable work on the manuscript for the book.

THE RESEARCH UNDERLYING THIS BOOK

This book is not based on guesses and hunches the authors might have about children, adults, or families. The book is based primarily on the timeless truth of the Bible and secondarily on high-quality research.

Research conclusions from many quality studies are summarized in the book, but by far most come from the National Study of Youth and Religion. Parents of all ages of children will find this research vital since all children are moving quickly toward the teenage years. Dr. Christian Smith, lead researcher on the project, provides the following overview.

The National Study of Youth and Religion is the most extensive and detailed national research study on the religious and spiritual lives of US teenagers to date, providing a depth of knowledge and understanding about the religious lives of US adolescents that was simply not available previously.

Research science has demonstrated that if a sample size is large enough and the selection of respondents is random—as is the case with our random-digit-dialing method—then responses from the sample will be nearly identical to the responses one would get from the entire population, that is, to what (in this case) every teenager and parent in America would say. The NSYR followed exactly this kind of careful methodology so that its findings can be assumed to accurately represent all the teenagers in the United States.

The survey—which was conducted in English and Spanish, as needed—gathered an immense amount of information on US teenagers' religious affiliations, beliefs, identities, experiences, practices, commitments, activities, congregations, and expected futures. The survey also collected a large amount of data about the teens' families, relationships with parents, schools, friends, neighborhoods, moral attitudes and actions, risk behaviors, dating and sexual experiences, emotional well-being, social ties to adults, and much more. No other existing national survey of teenagers comes close to having the detail of information on these aspects of US adolescents' lives, particularly their religious lives, as the NSYR contains.

The NSYR's first major findings are available in the book *Soul Searching: the Religious and Spiritual Lives of American Teenagers* by Christian Smith with Melinda Lundquist Denton, published in 2005 by Oxford University Press. Readers of *Parenting with Kingdom Purpose* can refer to *Soul Searching* for more in-depth reporting on the project and findings on which this book reflects and to which it responds.

CHAPTER 1

PASTOR, WHAT HAPPENED?

"PASTOR, I RAISED MY CHILD in a Christian home and in a Bible-based church, but now he wants nothing to do with the church. Doesn't the Bible promise that if I raise my child in the way he should go, he won't depart from it. Pastor, what happened? Why didn't that Bible promise work?"

I can't begin to tell you how many times I have heard this same sad story. The details may change, but the impact is always the same. The parents sitting in my office were devastated because their son not only wanted nothing to do with the church but had embraced a lifestyle that had broken the hearts of his Christian parents. The child that grew up in the influence of the church has now rejected the value system of his faith community and his parents.

Studies indicate that 70 percent of youngsters from evangelical churches drop out of church within two years of high school graduation.[1] How does it begin? What has caused this mass exodus? An even more important question is, What can we do about it?

What Happened?

I noticed that I hadn't seen John and Mary at church for several weeks. This was unusual. John was a new deacon, and Mary was involved in the small-group ministry of our church. I dropped them a note to tell them I had been missing them and that I was praying for them. I was relieved and delighted when I saw John and Mary with son Rodney in tow the next Sunday morning. They sought me out as they hurried away from church after Sunday School and prior to worship. They were clearly in a hurry.

"Hi pastor, sorry to be in such a hurry, but Rodney has a ball game. We are not going to be able to stay for preaching. We'll get the tape. I know we haven't been too faithful lately, but that will change this fall. Rodney made the all-star baseball team, and most of their games are on Sunday. Some take us out of town, and we have to leave on Saturday night. We hate we have to miss church, but this is a great opportunity we didn't think Rodney could miss. The coach tells us our son has real potential and may have a chance for a college scholarship if he focuses on his game. Who knows, maybe he'll get a shot at the pros some day. You know I could have had a shot if I hadn't been injured. Pray for us; he has a real talent from the Lord. We'll see you this fall."

I watched them as they sped to the car. These earnest parents wanted the best for Rodney. Or did they? Whose best interests were they seeking? Was this a dad who was living out his dream through his son? Was "best" being measured from a biblical standpoint or from the standpoint of the world? I didn't want to be judgmental, so I just watched and prayed.

Rodney did indeed show real talent. He progressed through the ranks of Little League, Pony Baseball, and American Legion Baseball, all the time making the all-star ranks. As he progressed, I saw less and less of John and Mary. After all, there were camps to attend and clinics that were essential to Rodney's development. He had to be seen by the coaches and the scouts if he was to have any chance to play at the next level. We stayed in touch, and they attended church once in a while. John felt he had to resign as a deacon since he had to travel so much with Rodney. It was, after all, important to keep the family together.

Rodney found it hard to make the transition from the children's ministry to the youth group. He didn't know the kids in the youth group very well and felt like an outsider when he attended. After all, he didn't have anything in common with the other youth. He saw them at school, but all of his spare time was taken up with baseball. He really wasn't interested in dating. He just didn't have the time right now. Baseball was his first priority.

The youth pastor, Mike, was surprised but excited that Rodney had decided to go to youth camp. Mike had worked to develop a friendship with Rodney. He had attended several of his games and had begun to spend time with Rodney in prayer and Bible study. He knew that Rodney found it awkward when the other youth talked about the Bible. After all, Rodney had missed much of the small-group study because of his busy schedule, and his parents didn't feel he should attend the Wednesday night youth explosion since he had little time to study, with practice every afternoon.

"Have to keep your grades up if you expect a college scholarship," they would tell him.

But Rodney was showing a real interest in spiritual things, and Mike was willing to go the extra mile. Rodney had confessed to Mike that he was getting a little burned out on baseball. He really wanted to develop some friendships among the youth group. Most of his peers on the baseball team were a little wild, and he didn't feel comfortable with some of the things he was doing to win their approval. They were both convinced camp would be a good opportunity to develop some good solid relationships with other youth and to grow spiritually.

Mike was speechless when John had made a scene at a parents meeting about the high cost of the camp. The youth pastor had explained that it included the cost of transportation and three meals a day for five days. The church was paying for all the other costs. He was surprised that John had reacted so negatively since he had sent his son to baseball camps costing many times what the youth camp would cost.

When Mike privately pointed this out to John, John exploded. "But baseball is my son's career. Camp is just fun and games!"

Mike tried to explain that while camp was indeed a fun event the focus was on spiritual development of kingdom youth.

John declared, "Rodney has plenty of time for that later. Right now he has to focus on getting that college scholarship!" The embarrassment on Rodney's face spoke volumes.

Mike was disappointed but not surprised when Rodney called to explain that he was not going to be able to come to youth camp after all. A big league manager had called and invited him and his dad to come to California for a ball game. They were going to get to sit in the dugout with the team. His dad believed this was too great an opportunity to pass up. There would be other youth camps. Sorry!

Mike didn't see Rodney much after that summer. He seemed to lose interest in spiritual things. The door of opportunity seemed to close.

Rodney's senior year was a disaster. He couldn't seem to find his stroke. His batting average suffered, and he couldn't seem to maintain any focus. His dad blamed it on poor coaching. He was also upset that Rodney had developed a relationship with a girl who was distracting him from his game. John had actually made an appointment to talk with me about Rodney. He and Mary had begun to suspect that this young lady was a bad influence on their son. They had smelled alcohol on his breath and were concerned that he had tried soft drugs. They were now desperate to know what they could do to help their son. He was becoming more detached from them and had no desire to come to church.

Disappointment grew as no professional team showed any real interest in their son. They rationalized their disappointment, arguing that a few years in college would do him a world of good. They were shocked when no scholarship offers were forthcoming. College coaches had apparently noticed the changes in attitude and focus. And there are increasingly large numbers of great high school players who will never play their sport at any higher level.

Rodney's life spiraled downhill when he went away to a small college where he was told he would have a good chance as a walk-on. He was cut after a few weeks, and in response his depression increased.

This is how the meeting in my office came about. What happened? Was God not faithful to his promise? Did these fictional parents actually raise their child in the way he should go?

THE STORY IS FICTIONAL; THE ISSUE IS NOT!

This story and the persons involved are all fictional, but the issue is not. We are losing our young people at an alarming rate. The culprit may not be baseball. It could be any other sport. It could be dancing, art, music, or any other activity that can become a focal point in the lives of our children. It may even be a lake house that was purchased with the intent of keeping the family together.

Before you miss the point of the story, let me make abundantly clear that I am not talking about keeping kids in church and out of sports. I am talking about balance and about kingdom focus. We will elaborate on kingdom focus in greater measure throughout this book, but at this point we must ask the ultimate question: What is my child's purpose on planet Earth? This question, of course, mandates that parents ask the same question of themselves. Until we understand ultimate purpose, we will continue to fail at life. Even if we succeed at sports or business, if we fail to accomplish that for which the Creator designed us, we will fail at life.

May I suggest a purpose statement that would reflect the clear revelation of our Creator? We were created by God in his image so that we might have a personal relationship with him. We were redeemed so that we might *advance God's kingdom by his power for his glory!*

I take this purpose from the concluding words of the prayer of Jesus as recorded in Matthew 6. If our purpose is to know God through Jesus Christ and then to advance his kingdom with every fiber of our being, are we doing our children a disservice if we fail to raise them in such a manner that they understand their purpose? If we are one day going to be judged by our Creator for the use of gifts and resources for his kingdom and we fail to teach our children this truth, are we doing them any favor?

To paraphrase a well-known quotation from the Bible, *"What if we raise our children to gain the world but in the process they forfeit their souls?"*

To make my point clear, let me go back to our fictitious story. I am not suggesting that Rodney's parents should not have encouraged him to nurture the gift he had for baseball. Rather, I am suggesting that this gift should have been nurtured in the context of a kingdom focus. His parents could have used his ability to talk about God's gracious gifting to him. They could have encouraged him to excellence based on God's desire that he could use this gift to honor the Father and advance his kingdom.

We need children who excel in every field—athletic, artistic, business—who see their gifts and vocation in the light of the overarching concern of the kingdom of God. This balance would help the parents to ensure that baseball or ballet did not become a surrogate god.

For example, Rodney's parents could have made decisions about church attendance that demonstrated to Rodney their ultimate concern for his spiritual development. I believe that God honors such a decision and that such balance may have actually enhanced Rodney's desire and ability.

THE FOCUS OF THIS BOOK

This book is intended to help Christian parents shape their children to be kingdom agents. The Christian community can ill afford to lose our young people if we are going to advance God's kingdom and thus accomplish the purpose for which we were designed.

This is not just a book about how to keep your child in church. Too many of our children and youth remain in church but still do not have a kingdom focus. They are not using their gifts for kingdom advancement, and they are not seeking their career with the overarching question, how can God use me in this place of service to advance his kingdom?

I know this may sound radical, but we *are suggesting that all young people should be raised with the conviction that they are to be missionaries and that their primary goal is to use their gifts and resources to advance God's kingdom so that every tribe, nation, and people group have the opportunity to respond to their rightful king.*

You may have detected that my definition of missionary is slightly different from normal categories we ascribe to missions. I believe that all Christians are called to be a missionary or kingdom agent in whatever realm they are called.

While we need what is normally termed "vocational missionaries," we also need athletes who see their sports arena as a platform for kingdom advance, doctors who see the hospital or clinic as their mission field, teachers who will go into our public schools with the passion of using their gifts to advance God's kingdom, artists and film producers who will use their creativity to advance God's kingdom in Hollywood.

Producing effective kingdom citizens should be the overarching goal of every Christian parent. Good parenting skills will be necessary to accomplish this task, and thus we will talk about great principles of parenting. However, our primary focus will be on giving practical suggestions about maintaining Kingdom focus. We will also put into kingdom perspective issues such as sexual purity, church attendance, Bible study, and quiet time. We have often taught these spiritual disciplines without connecting them to the issue of the kingdom, and many children have therefore seen them as legalisms that have little connection to the real world.

You will discover new ideas that will truly excite you. Have you ever thought of having a Christian bar mitzvah or bat mitzvah? We have borrowed a Jewish term because you may have been invited to attend such an event for the child of a Jewish friend. This home ceremony is held on the thirteenth birthday and would help our children understand what it means to advance toward manhood or womanhood. This could be combined with a beautiful True Love Waits ceremony which explains the value of sexual purity in the light of God's kingdom.

We believe every family should establish Missions Adventure Savings Accounts for each of their children (see chapter 9). These funds can be used for an extended mission trip a young person will take during high school or college. We also challenge parents to adopt a standard of living that provides resources for family mission trips and projects. These are the sort of practical suggestions you will receive with the goal of developing well-balanced and effective kingdom agents.

CHAPTER 2

THE KINGDOM OF GOD AND YOUR FAMILY

IN RECENT YEARS I have been challenged to read the Scriptures through with specific attention to the kingdom of God. I have been astounded, convicted, challenged, and transformed. In the first instance I was surprised to discover that it is a constant theme of both the Old and the New Testament. Somehow I had failed to notice that it was the focal point of the teaching of Jesus and the message of the early church.

Jesus' ministry was introduced by John the Baptist, a wilderness prophet. His message was simple but profound, "Repent, because the kingdom of heaven has come near!" (Matt. 3:2). We know today that he was heralding the coming of the Messiah. His pronounce-ment was pregnant with meaning as we will note in our look at the kingdom pattern from the Old Testament.

After Jesus was baptized by John, he was led by the Spirit into the wilderness. Among the temptations was Satan's offer of the king-doms of this world and their splendor. While Jesus rebuked Satan by insisting that one should worship and serve only the Lord God, the resolute focus of Jesus' ministry is found in Matthew 4:17: "From then on Jesus began to preach, 'Repent, because the kingdom of heaven has come near!'"

The implication is clear: Jesus began to teach and continued to teach about the kingdom. A quick glimpse at the Sermon on the Mount or the parables of Jesus will indicate that Jesus' primary focus was on the kingdom. A telling passage is Acts 1:3, which records Jesus' postresurrection ministry: "After He had suffered, He also presented Himself alive to them by many convincing proofs, appearing to them during 40 days and speaking about the kingdom of God."

My reading of the Bible began to challenge me to ask myself whether I had kingdom focus.

- ◆ What would it mean to be a kingdom person?
- ◆ How would I have to change my lifestyle?
- ◆ Was I willing to do so?
- ◆ How would it impact my relationship to my wife and children?
- ◆ Did I believe that kingdom living was the only route to true happiness and spiritual well-being?

Early in my Christian pilgrimage, I claimed Matthew 6:33 as one of my life verses. "But seek first the kingdom of God and His righteousness, and all these things will be provided for you."

- ◆ Do I seek first that kingdom?
- ◆ Do I believe that when I do, God will fulfill his promise to provide for me?

I began to notice that several of the kingdom parables deal with kingdom judgment. I realized that if my purpose on earth was to advance God's kingdom, I would one day be held accountable for how I had used the resources—time, gifts, sphere of influence, and money—to advance his kingdom.

The apostle Paul was reflecting this idea in 1 Corinthians 3:12–14: "If anyone builds on the foundation with gold, silver, costly stones, wood, hay, or straw, each one's work will become obvious, for the day will disclose it, because it will be revealed by fire; the fire will test the quality of each one's work. If anyone's work that he has built survives, he will receive a reward." I know that I want to live in such a manner that I can hear my heavenly Father say, "Well done!"

The challenge to become a kingdom person has been an ongoing one for me. Some days I think I am making progress only to find my old flesh still has an awesome hold on me. I long for the transformation that comes from obedience. I want to be a kingdom person, and that has become my quest. I hope you will join me. Before we can help our children have kingdom focus, we must begin the journey for ourselves.

Let's take a quick trip through the Scriptures to gain an understanding of what it means to be a kingdom people. For a more complete understanding of this concept, we recommend the study— *EKG: The Heartbeat of God.* This study can be experienced as a church or by your family.

THE EMERGING PATTERN

It is not trite to say that the Bible begins with the beginning *of everything.* God is the Creator of all that exists and as such is our rightful King. Not only did God create the earth, sky, and sea, and all that is in them, but he also created all the peoples of the earth. He is by virtue of creation the King of all nations and peoples.

The rebellion against the rule and reign of God in the heavenlies by Satan and the rebellious angels had an immediate impact on the earth and its peoples. Instead of joyfully serving the King, mankind has been in constant rebellion, a rebellion which has had a detrimental impact on the earth itself (cf. Rom. 8:20–22).

God's choice of Abram (Gen. 12:1–3) reveals his intention of using an obedient man and his descendants to bless all the families of the earth. Thus, the sovereign King selected a people to bless in order that all the peoples of the earth might, in turn, come to experience his blessing. The time of the patriarchs ends tragically with the chosen people in Egyptian bondage.

God's ultimate purpose is not thwarted by man's failure. God appears to Moses and tells him of his plan to redeem his people from Egyptian servitude. Moses is thrilled to hear that God has a redemptive plan for leading his people out of Egypt, but he does not see himself as a part of that plan. His excuses run the gamut of the familiar. "I'm not capable!" "I'm not able!" You know the list. We have all trotted them out from time to time.

Moses had missed the point that we all frequently miss. God had promised Moses that he would be with him and he would deliver Israel. Kingdom activity is always accomplished by God's power through his chosen people.

- ◆ Before you opt out of this kingdom parenting challenge, I want to assure you that God will empower you for kingdom activity.

Moses reluctantly leads Israel out of bondage and through the Red Sea, clinging to the promise that God would be with him and meet with him in the wilderness.

Here in the wilderness we find a clear and developing pattern of God's concern for the world and his desire to use Israel to reach the nations of the world. God first reminds Moses of what he had accomplished for them. "You have seen what I did to the Egyptians and how I carried you on eagles' wings and brought you to Me" (Exod. 19:4). Israel not only belonged to God by virtue of creation, but now they were his by virtue of redemption.

We cannot be a kingdom people or raise kingdom-focused children until we have a personal relationship with the King. Many church members who resist the demands to become kingdom-focused may be "cultural Christians" who have never been truly redeemed.

You may well remember that Paul calls upon the Corinthian believers to glorify God in their bodies because they had been bought with a price (1 Cor. 3:19–20). Those who have been redeemed are not their own; they belong to the Redeemer and King.

I don't want you to miss the wonderful assertion by God that he had brought Israel to himself. First, this phrase speaks of incredible intimacy. Israel was not redeemed from bondage because they deserved it but because their King desired for them to live in relationship with him. I am still stunned by the sheer magnitude of God's grace!

Second, the insistence that God brought them to himself speaks of mission. The understanding of God's grace should create in us the intense desire to fulfill the purpose for which we have been redeemed. We were redeemed with purpose—to join God in his mission to reach the nations.

The obedience factor! "Now if you will listen to Me and carefully keep My covenant" (Exod. 19:5a). In order to fulfill their mission, Israel must obey the covenant regulations of their rightful King. Their obedience is not a condition of their redemption; they have been saved by God's sheer grace, but their obedience is the key to their effective kingdom service. And so it is for us today.

Unique possession! "You will be My own possession out of all the peoples" (19:5b). Israel belonged to God. They were to be his unique and special possession. The word translated *unique* has the idea of a movable possession. There were two types of possessions in the portfolio of that day—real estate and precious jewelry. One was stationary, and the other was portable. Israel was the unique and movable possession of the King. He could move the people at his own design to enable them to be effective in his service.

This one idea, when fully comprehended, will radically change the kingdom effectiveness of our families.

◆ What would happen if each one of us saw the places where we go to work and play as the place where God has placed us for his own kingdom agenda?

◆ What if we looked for the kingdom potential in every encounter?

◆ Now what if every member of our families was trained to think in this way?

◆ Can you begin to imagine the sort of impact Christian families could have on their neighbor?

When we understand the implications of "movable possession," we will find that everyday life has kingdom implications.

A kingdom of priests! "And you will be My kingdom of priests" (19:6a). God had chosen Israel to mediate between sinful men and their rightful King. Simply put, they were to be his missionaries, his ambassadors. This theme of the priesthood of believers is more completely developed in 1 Peter.

By virtue of our redemption and our status as God's own possession, we are called and empowered to offer up spiritual sacrifices to the King of the universe. This insight transforms our giving, our worship, our good deeds, and our personal ministry. All of these are royal service offered to our King. As parents we have been given the responsibility and privilege of offering our children to the Lord and thus ensuring that they will fully serve him.

My holy nation! "And My holy nation" (19:6b). Israel was called to be a holy nation because the King who had redeemed them and called them was himself holy. If they were to represent the King on planet Earth, they must reflect his character.

We cannot ignore the call to holy living if we are serious about being kingdom people and nurturing kingdom children. This emphasis will help you teach your children about issues such as sexual purity, modesty in dress, and integrity in lifestyle. They are all related to our kingdom calling.

For all the earth is mine! The reference to the earth is often ignored or treated as only a geographical reference. I believe that it is a missiological command. Notice in the Exodus 19 text, it is closely connected to the phrase "out of all the peoples." God chose Israel to be a kingdom of priests among all the peoples of the earth. Israel had been redeemed by grace and with redemptive purpose.

We, like Israel, have failed to understand and accept our redemptive role among all the peoples of the earth. We have lost our passion for evangelism and our concern for the nations of the earth.

The Old Testament pattern is clear: God desires a people who will embody his character, embrace his mission to the nations, and obey his Word. God is looking for a family who will dare to embody his character, embrace his mission, and obey his Word. This will be the most exciting family adventure you have ever shared.

THE TRANSITION AND THE PROMISE

One of the most significant and yet overlooked texts of the Old Testament is Ezekiel 36–37. Israel is once again in captivity; this time Babylon is their place of captivity. How could God's chosen people be held captive by a people whose god is no god? This question must have been in the minds of the captives. God speaks to Israel through the prophet Ezekiel: "When they came to the nations where they went, they profaned My holy name, which the house of Israel profaned among the nations where they went" (Ezek. 36:20).

God had set Israel among the nations to embody his name by living holy lives. But Israel's disobedience and the resulting unholiness had profaned his name. Thus, the people of Babylon had concluded that the God of Israel was not as powerful as Marduk, the god of Babylon, or that he had failed to keep his promise. In any case the behavior of Israel and their captivity had caused God's name to be profaned.

We sometimes fail to realize that our behavior reflects on our Father.

- ◆ People today draw conclusions about the nature of God based on the actions and attitudes of those who belong to him.
- ◆ As parents we can help our children understand that their lifestyle is important to God and the basis for their witness.

God declares his concern for his holy name and his willingness to act to restore his name. I invite you to read the entirety of chapter 36. You will notice God's concern for the nations. Verse 23 is pivotal. God declares: "'I will honor the holiness of My great name, which has been profaned among the nations—the name you have profaned among them. The nations will know that I am Yahweh'— the declaration of the Lord GOD—'when I demonstrate My holiness through you in their sight.'"

This is one of the most important statements about missions in the Old Testament. God declares both a plan and a timetable for world evangelization. God's plan is to reveal himself through his people in the sight of the nations so that they will know that he alone is God. When God's people live in such a manner that they clearly reflect the character of God, *then* the nations will know.

Israel had failed to show concern for the nations; they had profaned God's name through unholy behavior, and they had disobeyed God's Word. They had *consumed* God's blessings, rather than *conveying* them. We cannot fail as Israel failed. Kingdom focus will enable us to help our children understand the importance of their behavior and will help us instill in them the desire to reach the nations. I hope you are beginning to see the potential that lies dormant in the Christian home if we can instill kingdom focus.

In the remainder of chapter 36, God declares his intention and strategy for revival. He speaks of cleansing, giving a new and responsive heart, placing his Spirit within his people, and making them fruitful once again.

Chapter 37 is the famous account of the valley of dry bones. God takes the prophet into a valley littered with dry and lifeless bones. He promises that these bones will live again. Sense the power of this verse: "So I prophesied as He commanded me; the breath entered them, and they came to life and stood on their feet, a vast army" (37:10).

In these later prophets we begin to see the focus switch from Israel to the Messiah and his remnant community. Israel, as a nation, had failed in their assigned mission, but God's plan to reach the nations had not been thwarted. He will raise up a remnant community who will join the Anointed One in fulfilling the redemptive plan of God.

I believe this promise points us to Jesus and his community of followers, the New Testament church. Thus the kingdom commission has become ours. This is the reason that Christian parents must nurture in their children a kingdom focus.

THE MESSIAH AND HIS COMMUNITY

The coming of the Messiah is declared in language that was certain to bring to mind the kingdom theology of the Old Testament. "In those days John the Baptist came, preaching in the Wilderness of Judea and saying, 'Repent, because the kingdom of heaven has come near!'" (Matt. 3:1–3). Matthew makes clear that Jesus' consistent message was the kingdom. "From then on Jesus began to preach, 'Repent, because the kingdom of heaven has come near!'" (Matt. 4:17).

It is noteworthy that the constant theme of the Sermon on the Mount is the kingdom. He declares that kingdom citizens will be salt and light to the world. Their righteousness will exceed that of the Pharisees. The righteousness of the Pharisees was an external facade, but the righteousness of kingdom citizens will come naturally/

supernaturally because it will be produced by the Spirit of God and thus give convincing proof that we are sons of our Father (5:45).

In Matthew 6, we discover that kingdom children live with singular passion—to receive the reward of their Father in heaven. This concern dictates the manner in which we pray, fast, and give. The prayer of Jesus is permeated with Jesus' concern that his followers hallow God's name, advance his kingdom, and accomplish his will.

Do you remember the threefold theme we found in the call of Israel?

◆ God was looking for a people who would embody his name, embrace his mission, and obey his word.

Jesus would fulfill the purpose of his Father where Israel had failed. Not only would Jesus fulfill this threefold task during his earthly ministry, but he would establish and build a new community to whom he would give his authority. To them (to us) would be given the keys of the kingdom of heaven (Matt. 16:19).

The mission and passion of the Messiah must be our mission and passion. The New Testament church is the primary instrument for kingdom advance on earth. When we turn to the book of Acts, we see the activity of the Holy Spirit in the expansion of the kingdom through the planting of doctrinally sound, biblically based, Spirit-empowered, New Testament churches is the pattern of kingdom advance.

Thus the Christian family must be fully involved in the church. We must lead our children to love the ministry of the church and to use their gifts in the service of the King through the church. The church and the family must be in dynamic partnership if we are going to be effective in kingdom advance.

THE POWER OF THE HOLY SPIRIT

Perhaps you are wondering if you are up to the task. Parenting is difficult enough without someone telling you that your primary responsibility is to instill in your children a passion for the kingdom. I have great news for you. You are not alone in this ministry. You have the resources of the Holy Spirit to enable you.

The early disciples were concerned about how they could carry on the work of Christ after he departed. Jesus promised that he would not leave them like helpless orphans (John 14:18). In fact he promises that they will have supernatural empowering. "And I will ask the Father, and He will give you another Counselor to be with you forever" (14:16). Now you can understand the reason that Jesus counsels his first disciples to wait in Jerusalem until the Holy Spirit comes upon them.

It's overwhelming for us to contemplate the idea that we can daily be involved in conversations and actions that will advance the kingdom and impact eternity. No kingdom task that you have will exceed that of developing kingdom passion in your children.

- First, you multiply your own effectiveness.
- Second, you ensure that kingdom passion will continue generation to generation.

THE REST OF THE STORY

Most of us are familiar with Paul Harvey's famous line. He sets the listener up with an intriguing story, and then he pauses and tells us that soon he will be back with the rest of the story. The rest of the story is found in the book of Revelation. Before you begin this kingdom venture with your family, it might be an encouragement to know that the King is triumphant.

We saw that ultimate victory prefigured in the resurrection. The resurrection of Jesus was the conclusive declaration that the Son was victorious. He had gone to the stronghold of the enemy and had emerged triumphant. At that moment Satan's days on earth were numbered. He has been defeated!

But he has not yet been banished from the earth. Since his ultimate weapon—the power of death—has been majestically overcome, he must now resort to deceit and deception, attempting to thwart the advance of the kingdom.

Even now—while not visible to our earthly eyes—Christ rules as King from his royal position. The sovereign Lord, the King of glory, is directing all of history toward one event—the judgment of the nations and the full and visible establishment of his kingdom. Our King is coming: "One like the Son of Man, dressed in a long robe, and with a gold sash wrapped around His chest. His head and hair were white like wool—white as snow, His eyes like a fiery flame, His feet like bronze fired in a furnace, and His voice like the sound of cascading water" (Rev. 1:13–15).

We look forward to a day when that kingdom will be complete. Then he will take the book from the Father's hand, and we will all listen as the elders sing, "You are worthy to take the scroll and to open its seals; because You were slaughtered, and You redeemed [people] for God by Your blood from every tribe and language and people and nation, You made them a kingdom and priest to our God, and they will reign on the earth" (Rev. 5:9–10).

As a parent you have the unique and holy privilege of preparing your children to become kingdom agents.

There is nothing you can do here on earth that will be more important than this task.

What profit would there be if we raise our children with the skills to gain the whole world and yet they lose their own souls?

It is our passion to rear kingdom children.

CHAPTER 3

THE KINGDOM PERSON

WHEN I ASK THE QUESTION, "Am I a kingdom person?" it forces me to ask several follow-up questions.

- ◆ What does a kingdom person look like?
- ◆ What does he or she do differently from the non-Christian or even the nominal Christian?

It seems to me that it is worth exploring these questions before we discuss how we can nurture kingdom-focused children.

Let me add my disclaimer at the outset. This list is by no means exhaustive, nor is it, in any way, inerrant. It is simply the outcome of our struggle to answer this question for ourselves and for others who are seeking to become kingdom-focused believers.

Second, let us be the first to tell you that we have not mastered the issue of kingdom focus. I have come to believe that it is a lifelong pilgrimage. But let me assure you that this is the most exciting pilgrimage I have ever undertaken. It fills every day with kingdom excitement. I find that I am looking for and anticipating kingdom activity. It causes me to reflect on my actions, words, and deeds. It is changing my priorities. It is forcing me to ask and answer lifestyle questions.

CHARACTERISTICS OF KINGDOM PARENTS

I don't have any simple formulas to give you, but I will give you some hints that I believe the Holy Spirit will use to inform your kingdom journey. Buckle your seat belt and get ready for the most exciting time of your life. Your life and that of your children will impact eternity.

A kingdom parent has a vital relationship to the King.

This would seem to go without saying, but nonetheless it is the essential point of departure. If you do not have a relationship with the King, every attempt to live a kingdom-focused life will be an excruciating and frustrating experience for both you and your children. Do you remember our brief look at Exodus 19? The kingdom commitment is preceded by the pronouncement that God had redeemed the Israelites from the bondage of slavery in Egypt.

Every human being, moms and dads, boys and girls, young and old, suffer from the bondage of sin until they are redeemed (or bought out of slavery). We were all created to live in dynamic relationship with God, but we have all sinned. Paul states it this way: "For all have sinned and fall short of the glory of God" (Rom. 3:23). Our sin created separation between us and holy God.

In order to redeem us from sin, God provided a sacrifice to pay the penalty of our sin. "He made the One who did not know sin to be sin for us, so that we might become the righteousness of God in Him" (2 Cor. 5:21). That verse refers to the sacrificial death of Jesus. Yet that offering must be received by turning from our sin and by receiving Christ as our Savior. "But to all who did receive Him, He gave them the right to be children of God, to those who believe in His name" (John 1:12).

Before proceeding any further, let's do a little spiritual checkup. Are you certain that you have received Christ as your personal

Savior? Have you acknowledged and turned from your sin to follow him? Have you actually asked him to come into your life and be your King? If not, why not do so right now? Just put the desire of your heart into your own words by confessing your sin and asking him to save you and rule over you.

If you have made that personal commitment and your children have not done so, ask the Lord to give you the opportunity to lead them to Christ. You are a kingdom person, and you can and should lead others to know the King. What better way to start than with your own children.

This is the beginning point for kingdom living. We are called to be kingdom people precisely because we belong to the King. We were created by him, and now we have been redeemed by him and for him. We are doubly his, and therefore our entire life is focused by the singular desire to please him. Paul encouraged the Corinthians to live in a holy way based on the fact that they have been bought with a high price, and therefore they no longer are their own property (1 Cor. 6:19–20).

A kingdom parent is passionate about worshipping the King.

Perhaps you are familiar with the Great Commission as it is stated in Matthew 28:19–20. It tells us that we are commanded and commissioned to make disciples of all the nations. What I find interesting is the often overlooked statement in verse 17: "When they saw Him, they worshiped Him." The first response of kingdom people is to worship the King. Listen to the psalmist: "Worship the LORD with reverence and rejoice with trembling" (Ps. 2:11 NASB).

Our earthly worship is the prelude to eternal worship of the King. The psalmist looks forward to the day: "All the earth will worship You and sing praise to You; they will sing praise to Your name" (Ps. 66:4). Want to take a glimpse into eternity? John sees thousands singing this song: "'The Lamb who was slaughtered is worthy to receive power and riches and wisdom and strength and honor and glory and blessing!' I heard every creature in heaven, on earth, under the earth, on the sea, and everything in them say: 'Blessing and honor and glory and dominion to the One seated on the throne, and to the Lamb, forever and ever!'" (Rev. 5:12–13). Just look at earthly worship as choir practice.

There are at least three ramifications to the matter of worship. First, as a kingdom parent you are granted the privilege of leading your family in personal worship. We sometimes think that the only worship we need occurs at church on Sunday morning. If your children don't learn to worship at home, they will often find worship on Sunday a boring intrusion into an otherwise exciting week.

Second, you must lead the way in prioritizing corporate worship. As a kingdom family, we do not attend worship from a sense of guilt but from a sense of joy. It is not an onerous burden but a priceless joy. Your attitude toward regular participation in worship at your local church will often ultimately determine the attitude of your children.

Finally, worship involves more than reading Scriptures and singing hymns; it also involves the giving of ourselves in service. "Therefore, brothers, by the mercies of God, I urge you to present your bodies as a living sacrifice, holy and pleasing to God; this is your spiritual worship" (Rom. 12:1).

A kingdom parent is passionate about prayer.

The sheer magnitude of understanding that we represent the King of kings brings us naturally to our knees. It is not insignificant that Jesus' disciples asked him to teach them how to pray. They recognized that prayer was the umbilical cord between the Father and the Son. The Son declared that he could do nothing apart from the Father (John 5:19). If the Son could do nothing from his own initiative, what can we do without constant communion with the Father?

The primary purpose of prayer is simply the joy of spending time with our Father. The sovereign King of the universe has invited you into his presence. He has given you a cell phone with unlimited minutes, he will never drop you off the line, and you don't have to run around saying, "Can you hear me now?" Every kingdom child has no greater joy than to spend time with his Father.

Second, prayer is the fast-forward button that advances kingdom activity into our everyday experience. This is why Jesus taught his disciples to pray, "Your kingdom come, Your will be done on earth as it is in heaven" (Matt. 6:10).

You may find it helpful to study *The Prayer of Jesus* by Ken Hemphill. A six-week study guide accompanies the book. This would be an excellent tool for family Bible study. Both can be obtained from any Christian bookstore, or you may find that your church may have both in the church library.

The prayer of the kingdom family will always include kingdom issues.

- ◆ You should always pray for the nations.
- ◆ Perhaps your family could adopt an unreached people group and pray for them to come to Christ.
- ◆ You should be praying for missionaries, pastors, and other full-time workers by name.
- ◆ Pray that the Lord will thrust out other laborers into the harvest.
- ◆ Pray for those who are being persecuted for their faith.
- ◆ Pray for all Christians.

A kingdom parent loves other kingdom people.

Jesus indicated that people would know his disciples because they love one another (John 13:34–35). If you look at the text, you will discover that this was not a gentle suggestion for kingdom people; it was a command of our King. "I give you a new commandment; love one another. Just as I have loved you, you must also love one another. By this all people will know that you are My disciples, if you have love for one another."

I realize that some Christians make it difficult for us to love them, but in truth we may all be a little difficult to love from time to time. God loved us while we were still ungodly. He has given us a model of love. John tells us: "We love because He first loved us. If anyone says, 'I love God,' yet hates his brother, he is a liar. For the person who does not love his brother whom he has seen cannot love God whom he has not seen. And we have this command from Him: the one who loves God must also love his brother" (1 John 4:19–21).

Parents must model this unconditional love in the home. When we talk critically about other believers, we tear down the desire to be in kingdom community.

It stands to reason that if we love one another we will seek to share life with other Christians in a community of faith. Kingdom living is such a challenging task that our families need a Bible-based, kingdom-focused church. The kingdom-focused church will by its very nature be an Acts 1:8 church. That means it will have a strategic plan to reach its community and will cooperate with other churches in reaching the surrounding community, North America, and the nations of the world. This strategic plan will of necessity impact the budget. Look to see that your church has allocated adequate resources to reach the nations.

A kingdom parent encourages the best in others.

No one modeled this kingdom characteristic better than our Lord. Do you remember that group of men he selected to be his first disciples? By the world's standards they were not a stellar group. Yet Jesus constantly encouraged them. He promised them that he would provide for their needs, and he entrusted his mission to them. When they failed, he not only disciplined them, but he restored them and gave them another chance.

Your first and foremost opportunity to encourage the best in others begins at home. Your child needs to head out into the world each day knowing that he or she is special to God and to you. In the beginning no one's evaluation means more to the child than that of mom or dad. While discipline may sometimes be necessary, you will make a far greater contribution to the kingdom development of your children by honest affirmation.

Help them discover their gifts and make much of their strengths. Unfortunately, we are often quick to point out the faults of our children. We need to excel on the side of underlining the strengths of our children. All children are different, but each is uniquely gifted.

Don't join the world by trying to force your child to fit a particular mold (Rom. 12:2). Let children be who God created them to be. Perhaps you had hoped for an athlete and you got an artist. Trust God! He created your son or daughter for his own purpose and joy. He never makes a mistake!

All your children will be different. Celebrate their uniqueness with them. Give them your permission to be all that God created them to be. Be their biggest cheerleader.

Your sons and daughters were created by a perfect, loving God who designed them for kingdom activity that was prepared for each of them uniquely before they were ever born. "For we are His creation—created in Christ Jesus for good works, which God prepared ahead of time so that we should walk in them" (Eph. 2:10). Wow! Your goal as a parent is to help your children discover and fulfill their kingdom mission.

Your children must know they have your unconditional love, and you must tell them in a language they can understand. (For specific guidance with this issue, see *The Five Love Languages* by Gary Chapman.) No one's opinion matters more to your child than yours.

By honest affirmation and support, you can help your children to develop a healthy and biblical self-esteem that is rooted in the understanding of who they are in Christ.

Your child must learn to appreciate his or her God-given uniqueness. Nothing will have a greater impact on your child's total development than a clear understanding of his or her unique design by sovereign God. This understanding will affect the thinking process of children, their emotional development, and their values, goals, and passions. Before your children can learn to take cues from the heavenly Father about their significance and purpose, they will look to you to help them hear from him. One of your most important kingdom goals should be to nurture your children to seek excellence from a kingdom perspective.

A kingdom parent looks at every event from a kingdom perspective.

This is truly one of the most exciting concepts of kingdom living. First we know that God has promised to work in every circumstance for our good. "We know that all things work together for the good of those who love God; for those who are the called according to His purpose" (Rom. 8:28).

This text does not suggest that God causes the evil things of our lives, but it does assure us that God is sovereign and he can take every event and work in it for our good. If you read further in that same passage, you will find that "his good" is to conform us to his Son. You can help your children see God at work in the good and bad. Help them to ask, "What does God want to teach me in my present circumstances?"

Second, we help train our children to see the kingdom activity all around them and to ask the Father to show them how they can join him in advancing his kingdom. I take my clue here from Jesus. In

John 5:17 and following, we read the story about Jesus healing a man on the Sabbath. He tells his detractors that the Son is not able to do anything on his own. The Son looks to see what the Father does, and then he does these things in the same way. "For the Father loves the Son and shows Him everything He is doing, and He will show Him greater works than these so that you will be amazed" (5:20).

You will have the privilege of helping your children see God's activity at their school, in the neighborhood, on the football field or the tennis court. God is at work 24-7, and he invites us to see and participate in kingdom activity. Nothing boring about this!

Kingdom parents seek first to portray God's righteousness through their behavior and to advance God's kingdom with all their resources.

"But seek first the kingdom of God and His righteousness, and all these things will be provided for you" (Matt. 6:33). This is a wonderful promise that we like to quote. Now we have the opportunity to embody this verse in our family life.

Our behavior and that of our children is important to God because we are his family and as such reflect his character. Our behavior is the salt that gives authenticity to our witness (light).

It is often challenging to teach children about the appropriate use of their resources—including time, talents, and finances. The kingdom-focused family has a natural teaching edge. If we are kingdom people, the King has rightful claim to all that we have. Thus we have a desire to use our resources to advance his kingdom.

It goes without saying that this must be modeled before it can be taught. This gives us the natural context in which to teach our children about tithing and serving others. It gives us a natural context to encourage them to do their best at school and at work. We represent the King and advance his cause in all that we do.

A kingdom parent desires a lifestyle that reflects his Father's character.

Simply put, this means that we will seek to allow the Holy Spirit to manifest his fruit in our lives and through our family. The Beatitudes become guiding principles as we hunger for righteousness and seek peace in our personal life and through our family. Your children should see this modeled in you and understand that it is a first priority for the family. Your children will generally prioritize what they believe to be important to you.

A kingdom parent has a passion to study and obey God's Word.

Bible study must be a priority in the home and the church. As parents you will want to ensure that your family attends a church that believes the Bible and teaches it effectively. Look for a pastor who preaches from the Bible. Find a church that provides small-group Bible study for every age group.

But Christian education is not primarily the responsibility of the local church. It is your responsibility. The church and the family must work in partnership, but you must take the lead. Establish a time of Bible study in your home. This may be awkward at first, but it will become more natural in time. There are abundant aids to help you in this task.

A kingdom parent is passionate about reaching the nations.

You cannot study God's Word without realizing that the King wants every nation and every people group to know him. You will have the privilege of instilling this passion in your children. This passion will be visibly manifested through personal witnessing and sacrificial giving to mission causes.

Have you ever considered a family mission trip? You can start right in your neighborhood. As your children mature, you can go further. Most missions-minded churches provide opportunities for children, youth, and adults to participate in mission activities.

We want to challenge every kingdom parent to set up Missions Adventure Savings Accounts for each child. This money will be set aside to fund an extended mission trip while a child is in high school or college. Some students will go for a summer, some a semester, and some a full year.

Also imagine the eternal impact if every family had a kingdom advance fund that would provide the resources for the entire family to participate in a short-term mission venture. I can't begin to calculate the possibilities.

It may be that God will call many of our children to the mission field as career missionaries. Such an event should be a joy for any kingdom-focused family. Paula and I are thrilled that our oldest daughter and her husband have felt such a call. We are equally delighted that our middle daughter and her husband have been called to serve through the local church here in North America. Further, we are equally thrilled that our youngest daughter and her husband are in the marketplace as kingdom agents. Kingdom parents should instill in all their children that they represent the King in whatever vocational arena they are called. The potential is staggering!

KINGDOM CHILDREN

Kingdom-focused parents will desire that their children place kingdom priorities first. Do your children know that their spiritual development is the most important thing to you? Have you communicated this and modeled it? Do you want to? We believe that you can, and we are going to walk with you on that journey.

We believe this is the most effective and balanced way to raise healthy, happy children. You may be wondering by whose authority we make such an assertion. By the King's authority! Remember that every Beatitude ends with the promise of happiness or blessing. Don't you want your children to be blessed?

This kingdom focus gives you the proper context to talk about spiritual, physical, social, and academic development. After all, we are told that Jesus grew in wisdom, stature, and in favor with God and man. We should desire nothing less than this balanced development for our children.

Kingdom focus allows us to teach our children to see their lives and resources in the larger context of God's kingdom activity on earth. It will help us all to see ourselves as pilgrims on this earth and subjects of a different kingdom. Ask yourself two simple questions: "If I know that everything on earth will one day be annihilated and that the only things which have permanent meaning are those invested in the kingdom of God, how would I live the rest of today? How would I nurture my children?"

SUMMARY

1. Kingdom parents have a vital relationship to the King.
2. Kingdom parents are passionate about worshipping the king.
3. Kingdom parents are passionate about prayer.
4. Kingdom parents love other kingdom people.
5. Kingdom parents encourage the best in others.
6. Kingdom parents look at every event from a kingdom perspective.
7. Kingdom parents seek first to portray God's righteousness through their behavior and to advance God's kingdom with all their resources.
8. Kingdom parents desire a lifestyle that reflects their Father's character.

9. Kingdom parents have a passion to study and obey God's Word.

10. Kingdom parents are passionate about reaching the nations.

CHAPTER 4

WHO CHILDREN AND TEENAGERS THINK GOD IS

EACH CHILD IS UNIQUE. American children and teenagers are all over the map in terms of religious experience. A few are devoid of anything that looks like personal faith while others have passionate devotion. Trying to lump them all together is simply a mistake.

Kingdom parents' greatest fear may be that their children will enter some awful rebellious period and reject the faith. That fear is mostly unfounded. (But an even greater danger exists. Keep reading.)

For the most part, children and teenagers tend to stay religious.

FACTS

- "More than four out of five teenagers report belief in God."[1]
- "About two-thirds of teens say they believe in God as a personal being involved in the lives of people today."[2]
- "Teenagers say: I believe in God (87%); I don't believe in God, but I do believe in a universal spirit or higher power (11%); and I don't believe in either (1%)."[3]

- ◆ "Seventy-one percent of American teens say they feel very close or somewhat close to God."[4]
- ◆ "Seventy percent of teens pray at least once a week."[5]
- ◆ "Only one in 20 religious teens reported dealing with many doubts about their faith in the previous year."[6]

Contrary to popular thinking, children generally do not become teenagers who are alienated from the church or its ministers and members. Seventy percent of attending teens say the church is a very good or fairly good place to talk about serious life issues.[7]

TRADITIONAL FAITH

Popular media portrays older children and teenagers as people who reject parents and faith as fast as they pierce body parts. Teenagers in movies view the church as a dinosaur and the faith of their parents as an emotional crutch. The only religious children and teenagers on the small or large screen are strange and unpleasant people.

This unfortunate portrayal flies in the face of the facts. Most US children become teens who embrace fairly conventional, traditional beliefs about religion and the supernatural. They are not stampeding to abandon the church or the faith they grew up with.

FACTS

- ◆ "US teenagers as a whole are not religiously promiscuous faith-mixers. Almost all US teens stick with one religious faith, if any."[8]
- ◆ "Children and teenagers are simply not hostile to or rebellious against religion generally or the faith tradition of their parents specifically."[9]

◆ "More than seven in ten US teens profess a belief in a coming judgment day when God will reward some and punish others."[10]

◆ "Only small minorities of US teens definitely believe in reincarnation, astrology, communicating with the dead, and psychics and fortunetellers."[11]

A FAITH SIMILAR TO THEIR PARENTS'

By the time they reach young adulthood, the great majority of children will have a faith similar to their parents. Of course there are exceptions but not many. Most parents who want to know where their kids are headed religiously just need to look in the mirror.

FACT

◆ "Only 6% of teens consider their religious beliefs very different from their mothers' and 11% different from their fathers.'"[12]

Most children become young adults with a faith similar to their parents. The question is, Is this good news or bad news?

THE MYTH OF INDIVIDUALISM

Nearly all children become teenagers who are profoundly individualistic. They simply do not realize the influence their parents and their church have in shaping their faith. They really do believe they are crafting a faith all on their own. (Interestingly, their parents think the same thing.)[13]

Actually, children and teens are just exhibiting typical American individualism.

Like the adults around them, they tend to believe that:

Each individual is uniquely distinct from all others and deserves a faith that fits his singular self. Each individual must freely choose his own religion. The individual is the authority over religion and not vice versa. Religion need not be practiced in and by a community.

No person may exercise judgment about or attempt to change the faith of other people, and religious beliefs are ultimately interchangeable insofar as what matters is not the integrity of a belief system but the comfortability of the individual holding specific religious beliefs.[14]

Parents grew up with Sinatra singing "I Did It My Way." Now their children have come to believe the same thing. "They have difficulty imagining how religion influences their lives because they tend to imagine that nothing influences them, at least without their final choice that it does so. The idea that one's life is being formed and transformed by the power of an historical religious tradition can be nearly incomprehensible to people who have allergies to outside influences."[15]

CHILDREN TEND TO BECOME TEENAGERS WHO BELIEVE GOD IS MOSTLY ABSENT

Today's teens tend to believe the central goal of life is to be happy and feel good about oneself. God does not need to be particularly involved in one's life except when he is needed to resolve a problem. (This issue will be addressed in depth in chapter 8.)

If children grow up to believe that God primarily exists to make them happy and if children usually adopt the faith of their parents, then parents need to ask hard questions about their own convictions.

RELIGION USUALLY IS NO BIG DEAL

Few children or teenagers feel a need to rebel against religion. Without realizing it, they have mostly adopted whatever faith was present in their homes. They think the church is a fairly OK place. They are glad God is around in case they need him. But generally, all this is no big deal. Religion is there; it just does not matter too much.

RESEARCH OBSERVATIONS

- "Religion is generally viewed by most teenagers—religious and nonreligious alike—as something that simply is, that it is just not the kind of thing worth getting worked up about one way or the other."[16]
- "Religion actually appears to operate much more as a taken-for-granted aspect of life, mostly situated in the background of everyday living."[17]

SUMMARY

The great majority of children grow up to be teenagers and young adults who:

- Are religious.
- Think the church is an OK place.
- Have religious beliefs similar to their parents.
- Think they developed their beliefs entirely on their own, never recognizing that home and church shaped almost all they believe.
- Think that God exists but that he is mostly irrelevant to daily life unless needed to solve some personal problem.
- Think that religion is OK but just not that big a deal.

Kingdom parents' greatest fear should not be that children will enter some awful, rebellious period and reject the faith. The greatest danger is that they will imitate that large body of adult Christians whose faith stays in the background of their lives and who believe God exists primarily to make them happy. That is the greatest threat to kingdom living and impact.

CHAPTER 5

INTRODUCING CHILDREN AND TEENAGERS TO GOD

NO PARENTAL DUTY MATTERS MORE than introducing one's children to Jesus Christ.

For every ten teenagers who graduate from high school lost, eight will spend eternity separated from God. In some homes the clock is ticking.

CHILDREN AND TEENAGERS HAVE NOT GRASPED THE BASICS OF SALVATION

Children who do not understand concepts such as grace and forgiveness cannot enter into a relationship with God through Jesus Christ. Even though most children and teenagers in the US are active religiously, the majority have failed to grasp the basics of the Christian faith.

◆ 13-year-old boy from Ohio
"God is just this big thing that's been there forever and controls everything, probably not personal, I don't know. [How did you come to that idea?] Ah, like I was just raised that way

40

I guess, and I guess I believe it till I hear another theory that's more reasonable or something, like from science."
- ◆ 18-year-old girl from Maryland
    "My beliefs are so wishy-washy, like I'll think something one minute, something else the next. I don't know what is most important, 'cause I don't really live by the Bible."
- ◆ 17-year-old girl from Illinois
    "I guess I'm a Christian, but I'm one of those still trying to figure everything out. I believe there's a higher power, but that's about all I know for sure."[1]

Researchers with the National Study of Youth and Religion counted the number of times teenagers being interviewed mentioned central beliefs of the Christian faith. The following list shows the number of teenagers who explicitly mentioned these concepts in their interviews. The teenagers were quick to mention general, somewhat hazy ideas about the personal benefits of being religious.

- ◆ 112 teenagers mentioned personally feeling, being, getting, or being made happy.
- ◆ 99 teenagers mentioned feeling good about oneself or life.

Note how many mentioned salvation or justification.

- ◆ 6 teenagers mentioned salvation.
- ◆ 0 teenagers mentioned justification or being justified.[2]

Such results brought the researchers to this conclusion:

"Very few of the descriptions of personal beliefs offered by the teenagers we interviewed—especially the Christian teenagers—come close to representing marginally coherent accounts of the basic, important religious beliefs of their own faith systems."[3]

Many children and teenagers who consider themselves religious have failed to grasp the central concept of God's grace.

RESEARCH OBSERVATIONS

- "Viewed in terms of the absolute historical centrality of the Protestant conviction about salvation by God's grace alone through faith alone and not by any human good works, many belief professions by Protestant teens, including numerous conservative Protestant teens, in effect discard that essential Protestant gospel."[4]

- "Only one out of every three teens accepts the biblical teaching that people who do not consciously accept Jesus Christ as their Savior will be condemned to hell. Millions of teens have bought into a works-based theology."[5]

- "Three out of every five believe that if a person is generally good, or does enough good things for others during their life, he or she will earn a place in heaven."[6]

Children who do not understand enough about grace for salvation also will miss the joy of living by grace.

TEACH CHILDREN THE BIBLE

Parents have the primary responsibility to teach their children the Scriptures that lead to salvation. Children not grounded in God's written Word will tend to make up their own beliefs about peace with God.

Parents must not depend on the church to teach children about salvation. The church is a great help, but parents are primary. With eternal heaven and hell hanging in the balance, parents must not leave anything to chance. They must teach Scripture about salvation until they are certain each of their children clearly understands.

- Failing to teach children what Scripture says about salvation is more dangerous than leaving an infant strapped in a superheated van all day.

- Failing to teach children what Scripture says about salvation is more dangerous than allowing toddlers to play near storm-swollen sewer drains.
- Failing to teach children what Scripture says about salvation is more dangerous than allowing children to ride tricycles in traffic.

After burying an infant they accidentally left in a hot car, parents then must face charges from the state. Society holds them responsible for gross negligence. In the same way parents will have to give an account to the eternal Judge some day. When parents try to say, "I was counting on those people at church to teach my child," they will find that statement inadmissible in court. Their responsibility for teaching their own children can be shifted to no other.

Here is the danger. When parents don't teach scriptural principles to their children, the children just make up ideas on their own. "Jesus prayed in John 17:17, 'Sanctify them in the truth; your word is truth.' Without knowledge of Scripture and theology, we are prone to create conceptions of God based primarily on our private spiritual experiences."[7]

- Parents who do not teach what Scripture says about salvation almost guarantee their children will simply make up their own ideas.
- Children who make up and trust their own ideas about salvation likely never will be saved.
- Children from Christian homes who never are saved spend eternity in hell.

Parents are not responsible for the decisions their children make about receiving or rejecting a relationship with Jesus Christ. Every person young or old stands before God on that issue. Children reared in warm, godly homes with full knowledge of salvation can choose to reject the Savior. But parents are responsible for parenting and communicating in a way most likely to lead to the conversion of each of their children. The stakes could not be higher.

WHAT CHILDREN AND TEENAGERS MUST KNOW AND DO TO BE SAVED

There are many ways to present the basics of salvation to a child or teenager. The following is one way a parent can lead a conversation leading to the prayer for salvation.

Are you a child of God? Have you been born again? If not, would you receive him as your Savior and Lord right now?

God created you in his image with the goal that you might know him as Father and live with him forever. "For God loved the world in this way: He gave His One and only Son, so that everyone who believes in Him will not perish but have eternal life" (John 3:16).

The only thing that separates you from God is your sin. "For all have sinned and fall short of the glory of God" (Rom. 3:23). "The wages of sin is death" (Rom. 6:23). This verse refers to spiritual death that if not resolved before physical death will result in your separation from holy God for all eternity.

The solution to your sin problem is found in the second half of Romans 6:23: "For the wages of sin is death, but the gift of God is eternal life in Christ Jesus our Lord" (Rom. 6:23). Jesus died for your sins that he might personally "bring you to God" (1 Pet. 3:18). This is why the apostle John could declare, "To all who did receive Him, He gave them the right to be children of God, to those who believe in His name" (John 1:12).

I believe with all my heart that you want to become a child of God. So first you must agree with God about your sin problem, committing that you will turn away from your sin. "Repent . . . and be baptized, each of you, in the name of Jesus the Messiah for the forgiveness of your sins" (Acts 2:38). This repentance is accompanied by conviction and confession. "If you confess with your mouth, 'Jesus is Lord,' and believe in your heart that God raised Him from the dead, you will be saved" (Rom. 10:9).

Confess this to God, then talk to him in prayer. Here is a simple guide to help you:

"God, I admit that I'm a sinner. But this day I turn from my sin to follow you. I believe that you sent Jesus, who died on the cross and rose from the dead, paying the penalty of my sin. I receive your gift of forgiveness and eternal life. In Jesus' name I pray. Amen."

If you sincerely prayed that prayer, you are a child of God.[8]

PARENT CHILDREN BY GRACE

The way parents parent also can help move their children toward a personal relationship with Jesus Christ. It is much easier to grasp the grace of God when children live with parents who relate to them in grace. Conversely, it is difficult to imagine that almighty God can be grace-filled when children seldom have seen that quality at home.

QUESTIONS

- ◆ Do you tend to hold grudges against your child, or do you continually clear the slate and permit fresh beginnings?

♦ Once a child has been disciplined after misbehavior, do you show your child warm and unfailing love?

"Grace is not so much what we do as parents, but how we do what we do. Grace is the best advertisement for a personal relationship with the living God."[9]

PRAY FOR THE SALVATION OF CHILDREN

Praying for the salvation of children is the highest privilege and gravest responsibility of a parent. Teaching children the basics of the faith is vital. Grace-filled parenting is vital. Inviting children to salvation is vital. But arching over all these duties is the duty to pray without ceasing.

The enemy knows the name of every child. The roaring lion intends to devour each one while on earth, and he intends to do his worst to each one for eternity. Christian parents absolutely must lift up their voices before daybreak, calling out to the Savior to rescue their children. Nothing else matters as much.

SUMMARY

♦ No parental duty matters more than introducing one's children to Jesus Christ.
♦ Even though children and teenagers tend to be religious, the great majority have not grasped the basics of salvation.
♦ Parents who do not teach what Scripture says about salvation almost guarantee their children will simply make up their own ideas.
♦ Children who make up and trust their own ideas about salvation likely never will be saved.
♦ Children from Christian homes who never are saved spend eternity in hell.

- Children more easily grasp the grace of God when they live with parents who relate to them in grace.
- Praying for the salvation of children is the highest privilege and gravest responsibility of a parent.

CHAPTER 6

THE ADULTS CHILDREN AND TEENAGERS NEED

RELATIONSHIPS ARE CENTRAL to making a kingdom impact on children.

Here is a fact that flies in the face of popular thinking: Children and even teenagers want genuine relationships with adults.

RESEARCH CONCLUSIONS

- ◆ "Most teens appreciate their relationships with adults and most of those who lack them wish they had such ties."[1]
- ◆ "Almost 75 percent of high school students say they get along very well or even extremely well with their parents or guardians. Overall, teenagers have a lot more admiration than animosity for family members, despite popular notions to the contrary."[2]
- ◆ "Asked how they'd like to spend more time, more teens chose being with their families over relaxing with friends, playing sports or anything else."[3]

Parents who want to have warm relationships with their children all the way through childhood and adolescence need to know their kids want that very thing.

CHILDREN AND TEENAGERS REFLECT THE ADULT WORLD

Some adults think severe adjustment problems are as much a part of adolescence as acne and changing physiques. Those adults are wrong.

Parents who have listened to the wrong voices are frightened to see their children moving toward adolescence. Even their adult friends have said, "You better enjoy those children while they're small. It won't be much fun when they hit those teenage years."

The notion that older childhood and adolescence brings on all sorts of problems is simply an urban legend.

RESEARCH CONCLUSION

- ◆ "Adolescence is not an inherently difficult period. Psychological problems, problem behavior, and family conflict are no more common in adolescence than any other stage of the life cycle. To be sure, some adolescents are troubled and get into trouble. But the great majority (almost 9 out of 10) do not."[4]

It is not the arrival of adolescence that produces problems within children. Those who do develop problems usually are just reflecting the fact that all is not well around them.

"An appropriate analogy may be the use of canaries by old-time coal miners to detect noxious fumes accumulating within subterranean tunnels. The bird's small size and physical fragility meant that it reacted to the mounting danger long before it was detectable to the miners. Children are society's canaries."[5]

Children and teenagers tend to reflect the adult world around them. Most children become teenagers who move through adolescence in good shape. Other children, also reflecting the world right around them, don't do so well.

THE FAITH OF THE YOUNG WILL MIRROR THAT OF KEY ADULTS

Children and teenagers need parents and other adults in their lives who have a genuine, vibrant relationship with Jesus Christ. They need adults to have such a kingdom faith because they will grow up to be much like them.

RESEARCH CONCLUSIONS

- ◆ "The majority of US teenagers seem basically content to follow the faith of their families with little questioning. When it comes to religion, they are quite happy to go along and get along. The popular images of 'storm and stress,' 'Generation Gap,' and 'teen rebellion' may describe the religious orientations and experiences of most teenagers of prior generations. But they do not accurately portray the religious realities of most teenagers in the US today."[6]
- ◆ "The evidence clearly shows that the single most important social influence on the religious and spiritual lives of adolescents is their parents. Grandparents and other relatives, mentors, and youth workers can be very influential as well. But normally parents are most important in forming their children's religious and spiritual lives."[7]
- ◆ "All research indicates that the most significant influence on the life of the teenager comes from parents. It is only when parents become uninvolved that their role of guidance is replaced by the gang, the peer group, or the friend at school."[8]
- ◆ "Though a child may be strongly influenced by his or her friends, the power of this peer group emerges as dominant

only when the relationship of love with parents is vastly diminished. Caring parents are the primary influence in shaping the moral values of their children."[9]

Knowing they are being imitated should motivate parents toward their own spiritual transformation and kingdom activity.

CHILDREN WITH SPIRITUALLY SHALLOW PARENTS

- ◆ Most children and teenagers reared in kingdom-focused homes become kingdom-focused young adults.
- ◆ Most children and teenagers reared in pagan homes become pagan young adults.
- ◆ Many children and teenagers reared in spiritually shallow homes become spiritually shallow young adults.

But not all do.

- ◆ A fair percentage of those reared in spiritually shallow homes walk away from the faith altogether as young adults. Watching parents who attend church but who do not center life on Christ and his kingdom confuses them and even turns them against the faith.

Bruce Wilkinson has it right: "The children of parents with (shallow) faith do not see the works of God or hear about the works of God. They may see parents who go through the motions of faith— going to church on Sunday most of the time—but they don't see evidence of that faith in their parents' everyday lives. . . . They don't see enough to cause them to value the faith of their fathers, and so they choose not to believe."[10]

GOALS OF CHILD REARING

Lost parents who are rather decent people generally want kids to become adults who:

- ◆ Are happy.

- ◆ Work hard and are financially independent.
- ◆ Live as good citizens and obey the law.
- ◆ Relate to spouses, children, and extended family in a warm, loving way.

Spiritually shallow parents would add they want their kids to become adults who:

- ◆ Are Christians.
- ◆ Attend church.
- ◆ Live morally.

Only kingdom-focused parents would add to these lists adult children who:

- ◆ Have as their highest life priority bringing glory to God.
- ◆ Commit themselves, their families, and their resources to expanding the kingdom of God by the power of God.
- ◆ Choose vocations, activities, and relationships so that all the nations of the earth might be drawn to God.

THE STAKES ARE HIGH

Most children of kingdom-focused parents become young adults with a vibrant, lifetime walk with God that is kingdom-focused. Many children of spiritually shallow parents become spiritually shallow young adults, and others walk away from the faith all together. The stakes could not be higher.

PARENT CHECKLIST

It is just human nature for most parents to say, "I guess I am doing OK spiritually, at least as well as most people." The following checklist, from T. W. Hunt's *The Mind of Christ*, can help a parent make a more objective evaluation of the progress he or she is making in spiritual transformation.

Spiritual maturity is too rich and complicated to be reduced to one pen-and-paper exercise. Even so, the following may give parents some hint about how they are maturing in Jesus Christ.

Danger: The parents who need this checkup the most will be the most likely to skip over it.

Parent Checklist

Worldly View	Christly View
I was born unlucky (or lucky).	God has had his hand on me.
I become bitter when one of my goals is frustrated.	In my setbacks I reckon on God bringing a greater good than I could have known otherwise.
I am rarely aware that a blessing actually comes from God.	I am aware that all blessings come from above.
My sins continue to plague me; I find it hard to go on.	After I sin, I ask God's forgiveness and move on in the confidence that I am a product of the future.
I cannot tell that I am becoming anything.	I can perceive process and progress in God conforming me to the image of Christ.
I live for the physical, whether it is sex, food, money, or position.	The values most important to me are definable but unseen, spiritual values.
I am a slave to my appetites.	My body is subject to my spirit. This may be expressed in my willingness to fast, pray, study, or witness.

My faith is controlled by what I can see.	I act on the belief that the physical world is under the control of the spiritual world.
My strength helps me meet the challenges of life.	I depend on the Holy Spirit to do everything I do.
I live for moments of gratification.	I live in a continuum of joy.
I am impulsive.	Although I have punctuation marks of joy or pain, my overall life continues to move toward the high calling of Christ Jesus.
I continue to grow more introspective as the years go by.	I find myself looking upward to God and outward to others more and more as the years go by.
My success is more important to me than anything else in the world.	I get joy in helping others succeed.
I get jealous when something good happens to someone else.	I enjoy seeing good things happen to another person.
I cannot sympathize with another person's hurt.	I weep with those who weep.
My life is dominated by short-term goals.	All my goals are subservient to the life goal of bringing the world to the feet of Christ.
My horizon is limited by time.	The only horizon I have is eternity.
Physical death is the end of life.	Physical death is the beginning of real life.[11]

Adults choose to grow in the Christian life primarily out of love for and obedience to God. Right behind that motivation is a desire to see children spiritually transformed as well.

Henry Blackaby has noted: "Each parent must build his or her family on the faithfulness of God. Therefore, let us resolve ourselves to be committed to living out each and every commandment of God's Word! God's commands to adults (parents) in Deuteronomy 6:5–7 are clear: 'You shall love the Lord your God with all your heart, with all your soul, and with all your strength. And these words which I command you today shall be in your heart; you shall teach them diligently to your children.'"[12]

RELATIONSHIP FACTORS AND SPIRITUAL IMPACT ON CHILDREN

Relationship factors between parents and children dramatically impact the degree of spiritual impact parents have. Parents who want more impact have to deepen relationships, but that can't happen until they get new insights into their own emotional makeup.

Nonreflective Parenting

Parents who are clueless about how their own personalities are impacting their children are destined to weak parenting.

CLINICAL OBSERVATION

- ◆ "The unwillingness of parents to look at the truth about themselves and their kids is called nonreflection. Operating nonreflectively (with little or no awareness of motivational forces within) is the single most important obstacle to effective parenting."[13]

Consequences of Nonreflective Parenting

◆ No Growth

Nonreflective parents seldom mature. They never get to know why they feel the way they do or how effective they could be.

◆ Automatic Responses

Nonreflective parents react to their kids on the basis of their own needs. Automatic responses are only temporary and usually have no long-term impact on [children].

◆ Distance

Nonreflective parents remain at an emotional distance from their kids. The parent-child relationship suffers.[14]

QUESTIONS

- ◆ Do you have a healthy curiosity about your own emotional makeup?
- ◆ Do you replay in your mind stressful times with a child in order to analyze how you reacted emotionally?
- ◆ Do you consider how your own childhood has shaped you?
- ◆ Are you willing to face potentially painful facts about weaknesses and emotional scars you may be carrying?
- ◆ Have you ever asked a close friend to help you see blind spots in the ways you respond to your child?

Several relationship factors make it even more likely that children and teenagers will embrace the faith and kingdom focus of their parents. Parents who are finding insight into themselves are ready to give attention to those relationship issues.

Heart Connections between Parents and Kids

Children and teenagers tend to embrace the faith of parents who have heart connections with their offspring.

A heart connection is the pipeline that connects the hearts of the parent and child. Through that pipeline spiritual impact flows from one generation to the next. Parents who keep that heart connection warm and strong usually see visible evidence that their faith and values are passing to their children. "And he will turn the hearts of the fathers to the children and the hearts of children to their fathers. Otherwise, I will come and strike the land with a curse" (Mal. 4:6).

RESEARCH CONCLUSIONS

- "When parent-child connectedness is high in a family, the 'emotional climate' is one of affection, warmth, satisfaction, trust, and minimal conflict. Parents and children who share a high degree of connectedness enjoy spending time together, communicate freely and openly, support and respect one another, share similar values, and have a sense of optimism about the future."[15]

- "Older children and adolescents who feel connected to their parents and siblings are less likely than their peers to suffer from emotional distress, experience suicidal thoughts and behaviors, exhibit violent behavior, smoke cigarettes, drink alcohol, or use drugs. They perform better in school, enjoy deeper relationships, and are well adjusted."[16]

- "The benefits of communications between parents and adolescents seem to depend on both parental values and the closeness between parents and adolescents. Without a close bond, the message—no matter how strong—stands less of a chance of being accurately perceived, accepted, and acted upon."[17]

- "Parent-child connectedness has emerged in recent research as a compelling 'super-protector'—a feature of family life that may buffer young people from the many challenges and risks they face in today's world."[18]

Josh McDowell summarizes the issue well: "Parents might be spouting biblical truths at their kids, but where's the relationship? Truth without relationship leads to rejection. We are losing our kids not because they don't hear the truth, but because the people speaking the truth haven't spent the time to build relationships with them."[19]

Broken Heart Connections

Children and teenagers not connected to the hearts of their parents begin a desperate attempt to meet their own emotional needs. Their emotional tank that should have been filled by parents is painful while empty. To make the pain stop, they create plans for filling the tank themselves. Unfortunately, their attempts to fill that tank while separated from parents and from God will be foolish. "Foolishness is tangled up in the heart of a youth" (Prov. 22:15).

A fourteen-year old girl might leave the house for school wearing a revealing outfit. Below the level of consciousness, she might be feeling: *I don't know what happened to my dad and me. We used to be so close. He would hold me and tell me I was beautiful inside and outside. Then he just seemed to get busier. When I started changing and growing up, he wasn't around so much, and he stopped telling me I was pretty. Sometimes I get so lonely, and other times I just need his hug. But the girls say there is a way you can make the boys hold you and tell you that you're pretty and even say they love you. And I will do whatever it takes to make that happen.*

CLINICAL OBSERVATION

- ◆ "Teens left to themselves will gravitate toward the view that trusting themselves and pursuing pain relief is a workable plan for their lives. The disgraceful results of such foolish beliefs are legion: drugs, dropping out of school, family conflict, and so on."[20]

Heart Connections Can Weaken with Age

Parents who are not vigilant may find that heart connections with their children weaken as those children grow.

RESEARCH CONCLUSIONS

- "Youth and parents, independent of one another, both reported less unity and closeness as the children moved in age from fifth to ninth grade. There was a discernible decline in parental harmony, communication, parental control, and expressions of love as children approached adolescence."[21]
- "The percentage of parents expressing verbal affection ('I love you') went from 50 percent for fifth graders to 30 percent for ninth graders. The percentage of parents showing physical affection (hugs or kisses) dropped from 73 percent to 40 percent within the same age-group."[22]

Injuries to Heart Connections

The beliefs, values, and ethics of parents positively influence the majority of children and teenagers. Similarly, the majority want to spend positive time with their parents. But a smaller group are a clear exception. They want neither the opinions nor the presence of their parents. What went wrong?

Many of these students push parents away in order to protect themselves from more hurt. They have been abandoned emotionally by parents preoccupied with career, income, self-fulfillment, failing marriages, new romances, adult recreation, community involvement, or even church busyness. Some live in the slums with single moms working two jobs, but even more have homes on the golf fairway.

Counselors call these children and teenagers disconnected, wounded, or kids with emotional tanks running on empty. Unless something changes quickly, they will reject the faith, go off the deep end in terms of lifestyle, and spend their lives distant from parents.

Bruce Wilkinson has observed:

- "Injured relationships account for the overwhelming majority of long-term parenting problems in Christian families.

- When biblical guidelines for raising godly children have been applied and don't seem to be working, injured relationships are usually the culprit.

- Injured relationships are the major, hidden force that drive our children away from (kingdom) living, and sometimes from the faith altogether.

- If your child has received a heart wound from you or his other parent (or both), he will intuitively put up dividing walls, remaining aloof regardless of what you say or do.

- I must tell you that the most tenacious wounds are often the most deeply buried ones, the least expected, the most easily dismissed."[23]

QUESTIONS

1. If your child or teenager is genuinely pushing away your convictions and values and genuinely does not want to be around you, might he or she be reacting to emotional neglect?

2. Is it possible your drive to provide your child with economic advantages has caused you to be physically absent and emotionally drained and distant?

3. Is it possible your stressful marriage, new romance, or adult friendships have left you with little time or energy for your children?

4. Are you aware that if your child is emotionally abandoned by you, he or she almost certainly will reject your faith, make terrible lifestyle choices, and drift even further away from you as an adult?

5. To keep from losing your children, are you and your spouse
    willing to consider making life-altering changes related to
    absence from the home and reserving emotional warmth
    for them?

6. With Scripture as your guide and God as your strength,
    will you commit to doing whatever it takes to provide your
    children with the unconditional love, sense of significance,
    and emotional security they must have to prosper?

7. If there is the need, will you do whatever it takes to heal
    an injury your child may be carrying from you?

Inoculating or Restoring Heart Connections

Parents and teenagers who have strong heart connections can
inoculate those relationships to make drifting apart unlikely. Parents
and teenagers who already have started drifting apart can restore the
relationship they have lost.

The book *30 Days: Turning the Hearts of Parents and Teenagers
Toward Each Other* guides families through a powerful experience
that builds or restores heart connections. Each evening a parent and
teenager go to a room with a closed door and pull chairs near each
other. They light a candle and turn off the other lights. They break
the seal on the *30 Days* envelope for that night. For the first time
they see the five cards for that evening. Some cards go to the
teenager and some go to the parent. By following the instructions on
the cards, the parent and teenager say and do those things that have
the most powerful potential to turn their hearts toward each other.

Also, each evening they find a fresh way to pray together.
Many thousands of families have seen dramatic changes in relationships through this experience. (For more information, go to
www.josiahpress.com.)

Unfailing Love from Parents

Children and teenagers tend to embrace the faith of parents who show them unfailing love in ways they can understand.

When a vibrant heart connection is in place, unfailing love flows from parent to child. Parents who love their children without conditions are modeling Father God who shows that same grace to his children.

CLINICAL OBSERVATIONS

- ◆ "Below the waterline, teens are asking, 'What kind of person do I have to be to get someone to want and love me?' The wise parent's answer is, 'You don't have to be anyone but yourself to be loved and valued.'"[24]
- ◆ "Because the most powerful need of children is for love, adults can be tempted to withhold love to control behavior. But emotionally blackmailing kids by threatening to withhold love does great damage to the trust essential for positive relationships."[25]

Gary Chapman has noted: "I deeply believe that the most important influence on the teenager's mood and choices is parental love. Without a sense of parental love, teenagers are more prone to being swept along by the wind of confusion. . . . In contrast, teenagers who genuinely feel loved by their parents are far more likely to respond to the deep longings for community, to welcome structure, to respond positively to guidelines, and to find purpose and meaning in life."[26]

Some parents did not grow up in loving, affectionate families. That is unfortunate, but it is not an excuse for withholding love and affection from one's children today. Parents absolutely must show warmth whether it is natural or not.

QUESTIONS

- When you as an adult are being as sinful as you ever get, does God withdraw his love from you? (You may break the heart of God, and you certainly will experience his discipline, but his love for you is unfailing.)
- Are you willing to parent your children the way your heavenly Father parents you?
- Do you withdraw the warmth of your love as a way to punish a disobedient child? In other words, do you become cold and distant to show your child you are displeased with bad behavior? (If love is withdrawn after bad behavior, it is not unfailing love.)
- Do you tend to pour on the warmth of your love as a reward when your child accomplishes something important to you? (If love has to be earned, it is not unfailing love.)
- Do you, every day of your life, say the words "I love you" to each of your children? (If you can't get the words out of your mouth, you need professional help.)
- Will you respond to the bad behavior of a child with your discipline while the warmth of your love is unfailing?

Good news: "An attitude of unconditional (love) tends to pull kids towards the home and ultimately toward God."[27]

A Biblical View of Self for Parents

Children and teenagers tend to embrace the faith of parents who have a healthy, biblical view of self.

An unbiblical view of self among parents can undermine spiritual impact in the home. Here are just a few illustrations.

1. Parents with a low, unbiblical view of self tend to become destructively angry when their children directly disobey them.

Just below the level of consciousness, a parent might be thinking: *I have almost no authority in life. At work everyone tells me what to do, and I get to boss no one. I really counted on my child being the one person who would make me feel powerful. But now this person one-third my age is telling me he has no intention of doing what I say. He is going to get the full force of my rage for taking away my last hope for power.*

2. Parents with a low, unbiblical view of self often try to live vicariously through their children.

Some parents have a desperate desire to relive through a child that brief moment during their own childhood when some activity or accomplishment propped up their sense of significance. Of course, for this plan to work, they have to force a child who may not have their interests or abilities to play that role. Other parents take a different tack. Instead of forcing a child to replay their moment of glory, they try to force one to make up for what they never achieved. The "ugly duckling" might build her entire life around helping her daughter become the belle of the ball.

3. Parents with a low, unbiblical view of self become hopeless and depressed when their children don't turn out well.

Counting on parenting success to validate their worth and value, they fall apart when they seem to have failed. Healthy parents experience honest grief when children struggle. Parents with low self-esteem experience depression and hopelessness instead.

A healthy, biblical view of self emerges when parents embrace the fact that they were:

- ◆ Each designed by God.
- ◆ Redeemed by his blood.
- ◆ Wooed to salvation by his Spirit.
- ◆ Placed on earth with a mission given no one else.
- ◆ Filled with all the gifts and abilities needed to complete that mission.

Appropriating that truth leads to godly living and wonderful parenting.

Open Communication

Children and teenagers tend to embrace the faith of parents who maintain open communication with them.

"Counsel in a man's heart is deep water; but a man of understanding draws it up" (Prov. 20:5).

Children and teenagers want communication with parents.

◆ "Reject the myth that noncommunication is normal for teenagers. You've heard it said over and over: 'Teenagers just don't talk to their parents. You'll have to accept the fact that they clam up and hole up in their rooms.' It may be common for teens to avoid talking to you, but it's not normal. Teenagers long for a caring adult to hear and understand their thoughts, dreams, and ideas."[28]

Children and teenagers are open to deep communication only for brief times.

◆ "There is an interesting phenomenon with children called the open window that is often missed by parents who are too busy. Open windows are moments in time when your children will invite you in to their private world."[29]

The evening meal is a vital time for communication.

◆ "Researchers found the frequency of family meals was inversely associated with tobacco, alcohol, and marijuana use; and low grade-point average, depressive symptoms, and suicide involvement. So the more times a teen reported sitting and eating with their family the less likely they were to report substance abuse, mood disorders, or poor academic performance."[30]

◆ "The sobering truth is that you can be in the same house, the same gym, but be clueless about what's really going on in your child's life."[31]

PRACTICAL SUGGESTIONS

◆ Listen to them (see James 1:19).

◆ As they approach adolescence, begin to give them opportunities to share their hearts with you (see Rom. 12:15).

◆ Listen to their feelings without immediately giving them the correction you think they need (see Prov. 18:13).

◆ Be trustworthy with their hearts. None of us is willing to risk sharing vulnerable feelings with someone who will attack us with what we share.

◆ Share with them weaknesses or struggles you are having in your own life.[32]

TO INVITE CONVERSATION

Sitting down just to talk can be too intense or awkward. So add a comfort cushion like these:

◆ Work on a project together.

◆ Take a walk.

◆ Use car time.

◆ Use a look of ultimate love. When you invite your teen to talk, include a no-matter-what look of unconditional love. Even if your teen says nothing, you will have made a connection.[33]

Words of Encouragement and Affirmation

Children and teenagers tend to embrace the faith of parents who communicate their significance and provide encouragement.

"Life and death are in the power of the tongue" (Prov. 18:21).

"No rotten talk should come from your mouth, but only what is good for the building up of someone in need" (Eph. 4:29).

WAKE-UP CALL

◆ "Listen to yourself—do you communicate to them that you are never completely pleased, satisfied, or content with them or their efforts? Is it possible your careful scrutinizing has left them feeling that they can never measure up, like they can never succeed?

♦ Consider that your adolescents may be resistant to your leadership, only because they felt so rejected by you that they gave up trying to please you.

♦ Many middle-aged adults still crave their parents' approval. Do you want your children to be your age and still be waiting for you to say, 'I'm proud of you'?

♦ Consider that many kids who fail to find their parents' acceptance will welcome it from the first group or individual who offers it.

♦ Remember that we are drawn to those who like us but have little time for those who continually criticize us."[34]

CLINICAL OBSERVATION

♦ "Affirmation is a much greater motivator than guilt and shame.

♦ One model of communication says it takes nine affirming comments to make up for just one critical comment.

♦ Sure our teens need discipline, and you should discipline with consistency, but they also need words of encouragement.

♦ They will respond much greater to a compliment and affirmation than a negative, angry putdown."[35]

LIFE WORDS AND DEATH WORDS

♦ "Life words are words, phrases, and questions that encourage teens to share about their inner worlds. Life words help kids to understand their own behavior. Life words communicate unfailing love and acceptance.

♦ Death words are negative words that kill the parent-teen relationship. Usually spoken in anger, death words leave kids feeling discouraged and confused. . . . [Kids] usually feel . . . hurt, hesitant, and often angry when they hear death words. Parents always forfeit influence whenever they speak death words."[36]

TONE OF VOICE

Parents may not realize their words and their tone of voice may be continually critical and sarcastic. Here is a test.

- ◆ When a fellow employee at work disappoints you, do you use the same sarcastic or critical tone of voice you use with your children?
- ◆ When a minister or some other visitor is in your home, does your way of speaking to your children improve?

Parents know that if they become sharp tongued or sarcastic to their adult friends or coworkers, those relationships instantly will begin to cool. Why should parents expect anything different at home?

Affirming in the Presence of Others

Notice how differently two parents might handle the following situation. Parent and child are standing side by side at church as a minister approaches.

Minister: "Oh Mrs. Smith, you would have been so proud of your daughter on our mission project. She was up there hammering shingles with the best of them. I was so impressed with her desire to serve those impoverished families."

Foolish Parent: "All I can say is, you leaders must be miracle workers to get that kind of work out of her. It is all I can do to get her to clear a path through her bedroom."

Minister: "Oh Mrs. Smith, you would have been so proud of your daughter on our mission project. She was up there hammering shingles with the best of them. I was so impressed with her desire to serve those impoverished families."

Wise Parent: "That doesn't surprise me at all. Sarah has a warm heart for people in need, and she can really pour herself into any project she believes is important."

Question:

How many days, months, or years has it been since you built up your child in the presence of a significant adult?

Blessings and affirmations for a child double in impact when they are given in front of significant others. It is foolish to miss one opportunity to do so.

BOTTOM LINE

Kingdom parents honor God by recognizing that his worth is beyond any price. Similarly, parents honor children by considering them to be special gifts God has entrusted to them, as the Scriptures declare. Parents should remind children daily how valuable they are.

Focused Time with Children

Children and teenagers tend to embrace the faith of parents who spend focused time with them.

CLINICAL OBSERVATIONS

- ◆ "One of the main precipitating factors in teen suicide is a lack of time spent with one or more parents and the resulting feelings of abandonment. Kids interpret lack of time or intimacy as rejection.
- ◆ Many parents who were actively involved in their child's life during the early years withdraw when their child becomes a teenager. This is a mistake. It's just as important for parents to be involved now—maybe even more so.
- ◆ Parents who are around little because of divorce, work schedules, etc., jeopardize the teenager's sense of feeling connected

to parents. It is a simple reality that for a teenager to feel connected and thus loved by the parents, they must spend time together. The teen who feels abandoned will wrestle with the question, 'What's wrong with me that my parents don't care about me?'"[37]

♦ "According to those who study them, over-scheduled lives can damage marriages, lead stressed and overwhelmed children down the road to depression, and cause adolescents to turn to drugs, alcohol, and sex."[38]

Parents daily must balance the attention needs of their children and the parents' desire for

♦ Personal peace
♦ Pleasure
♦ Possessions

Overextending at Work

Some parents convince themselves that they are overextending their hours at work in order to provide good things for their children. If they were more honest, they might acknowledge that the real attraction is the ego boost they get from vocational accomplishments. That ego boost has to be weighed against the harm that comes to children when a parent is absent too often.

A second motivation for overextending at work centers on the desire for a higher standard of living. Families in apartments want their own home with siding. Families with homes with siding want a brick home. Families with brick homes want a home in a gated community. Families in gated communities want a mansion on the fairway.

A desire to improve one's financial situation is not necessarily wrong. It is biblical to work hard and with excellence. Hard work with quality often is rewarded financially. Biblical qualities such as honesty and treating others with fairness are valued by many companies and thus may lead to financial advancement. Christian character qualities may equip a leader to manage well with an increasing span of responsibility, leading to financial progress.

A parent can work only so many hours each week without doing damage to the family. Within that number of hours, the parent can work "as unto the Lord," even pursuing financial progress and professional achievement.

Parents cross the line from biblical obedience to disobedience when their desire for advancement leads to overextending work hours. It is impossible to justify work hours that leave children (or spouses) empty. No financial benefit for the family can make up for children who receive too little focused attention, too few heart conversations, too little time-sharing activities, too little discipline, and too little spiritual instruction.

Here is a declaration two kingdom parents might make that flies right in the face of the so-called "American dream."

"We sometimes are frustrated with our modest house and neighborhood. If both of us stretched ourselves to the limit, we can see a way we could get into that better neighborhood. But while children are in our home, we are choosing something better. We would rather have a modest home that is filled with laughter, long talks, and relaxed evenings. We would rather see our children leave for school each morning with their emotional tanks brimming full. We would rather have time to gather at the end of the day to pray and speak of the things of God. We will enjoy dreaming of better neighborhoods out in the future, but today we want something far better."

Second Wage Earner

Most second wage earners enter the workplace to provide a higher standard of living for the family. It is reasonable to ask whether that slightly better standard of living is worth elevated family stress and less focus on children.

A second income only slightly raises the standard of living due to higher income tax brackets for both workers, work clothes and dry cleaning, dining out, lunches, fast food, home maintenance that dual-career couples often pay someone else to do, gas, and child care. One study found a $30,000 second income resulted in about $5,400 of actual monetary benefit to the family.[39]

When both parents work outside the home, both arrive home with batteries drained. Even though tired, both must give much of the evening to home management duties.

Children needing well-crafted discipline need a parent who has strength reserves for the task. Children needing someone to listen to their hearts in conversation need a parent with time and strength. Children who need both the structure and the guidance to do multiple homework assignments need a parent who has something left to give. Children who need calm dinners with laughter and conversation need a parent who has the time and strength to prepare for this every day.

Home Alone

Middle schoolers home alone after school are at special risk. In fact, they are at higher risk than older grade schoolers home alone. The home has replaced the auto as the most common location for first sexual encounters. First drug experimentation often occurs in the after-school hours, including inhaling household products. The dark side of the Internet has added dangers, with older children and teenagers usually one step ahead of whatever safeguards the parents try to impose. Children and teenagers who struggle with depression often face their greatest struggles when home alone. The presence of a parent after school not only fills emotional tanks; it can save the lives of children.

THE BOTTOM LINE

Some young couples are honest enough to acknowledge that they prefer professional and economic advancement to child rearing. One might question their decision not to have children on other grounds, but at least no children get hurt in the process.

Christian couples who decide to have children also must decide that for two or three decades of their lives, those children will be a life priority. Parents acknowledge:

1. We must have time to keep our relationship with God warm, fresh, and growing.

2. We must have time to meet the most basic physical needs of our children, including the vocational time it takes to be able to feed, shelter, and clothe them.

3. We must have time to meet all the spiritual, emotional, and relational needs of our spouse and children.

4. We must have time to accomplish that part of God's unique calling and mission for our lives that falls outside the home.

5. Once we have created a way of life that consistently and completely is meeting those four needs, we can consider what time is left for vocational and economic advancement.

Children don't become kingdom kids because they go to better schools, wear the best labels, or have more elaborate vacations. Children become emotionally and spiritually vibrant young adults because, in part, they spend powerful hours enjoying the focused attention of their parents. God is calling many families to limit the time one or both parents spend working outside the home to rear emotionally and spiritually vibrant kingdom children.

Overextending in Extracurricular Activities

Extracurricular activities should build emotionally and spiritually vibrant children and teenagers. When extracurricular activities take so much time that they make time with parents and family impossible, then they no longer are accomplishing their purpose. Just because being on one team is good does not mean being on three teams is better.

Parents who push their children to overextend in activities need to ask themselves hard questions.

- ◆ Am I pushing my child to overextend in hopes he will excel because I need to prop up my weak self-concept by living vicariously through the successes of the child?
- ◆ Am I pushing my child to overextend in hopes that she will win a major scholarship and thus allow me to hold on to college savings?

BOTTOM LINE

Here is the critical question:

- ◆ Has your family's schedule become so crazy that too few minutes are available for focused attention on children, quiet conversations, and even spiritual leadership?
- ◆ If your answer is yes, will you take a ruthless inventory to discover what is pulling family members apart evenings and weekends?
- ◆ Once you discover what is causing the craziness in schedules, will you ask for God's leadership in knowing what changes must be made?

Some say a sign of insanity is continuing to do what you have been doing but expecting a different result.

If families don't have time to keep their hearts connected, something needs to change immediately.

Warm, Intimate Marriages

Children and teenagers tend to embrace the faith of parents in a vibrant, lifetime marriage.

Children and teenagers tend to embrace the faith of parents who surround them with emotional security. Believing the marriage of parents will last is a primary source of that emotional security. Questioning whether the marriage will last robs children of that security.

RESEARCH CONCLUSION

"The research evidence from a number of studies is overwhelming. Parental harmony contributes enormously to the emotional health of children, whereas marital conflict is devastating in its long-lasting effects."[40]

In this instance, it does not matter whether parents think their marriage will make it. The children come to their own conclusions. When they hear muffled shouts coming from the master bedroom, or they detect icy stares between parents at dinner, or they see touching and flirting become rare, they make their own evaluation about whether the marriage will make it. If the children decide the marriage is not well, their emotional security vaporizes, and their behavior becomes consistent with insecurity.

Parents who have been wounded by a spouse may no longer feel motivation to rebuild romance from the perspective of his or her own needs. But kingdom parents find the motivation to rebuild what has been lost for the honor of God and for the good of their children.

Parents who are warm, romantic, and even appropriately affectionate in front of their children are taking a giant step toward rearing kingdom kids.

Parenting with Grace

Children and teenagers tend to embrace the faith of parents who relate to them with grace.

◆ If you carry unrelenting resentment toward them, forgive them. . . . Don't bring up old offenses and repeatedly scold them for them.

"[Love] . . . does not keep a record of wrongs" (1 Cor. 13:5).

◆ Give them continued fresh starts. Don't think the worst of them, continually guessing their motives to be evil. Love hopes the best. Give them the benefit of the doubt.

"Be kind and compassionate to one another, forgiving one another, just as God also forgave you in Christ" (Eph. 4:32).

◆ Ask forgiveness of them for your resentment.

"So if you are offering your gift at the altar, and there remember that your brother has something against you, leave your gift there in front of the altar. First go and be reconciled with your brother, and then come and offer your gift" (Matt. 5:23–24).

◆ Do not justify your anger.

"For man's anger does not accomplish God's righteousness" (James 1:20).

"And fathers, don't stir up anger in your children, but bring them up in the training and instruction of the Lord" (Eph. 6:4).[41]

Sensitive kids who mess up and are disciplined then want to restore their relationship with parents, but they don't know how to do this. They don't know how to get the warmth back. Parents who parent with grace must take the initiative to communicate that all is well and the relationship is restored.

Adults Outside the Family

Adult relationships outside the family can have a kingdom impact on children and youth.

Older children and teenagers spend the great majority of time outside the home with people almost exactly their age. School, team sports, extracurricular activities, and even church can mean they spend most hours outside the house with people only a few months different in age. That is not necessarily a good thing.

RESEARCH CONCLUSIONS

- ◆ "Numerous researchers have demonstrated the protective impact of extra-familial adult relationship for young people, including other adult relatives, friends' parents, teachers, or adults in health and social service settings, among others. This sense of connectedness to adults is salient as a protective factor against an array of health-jeopardizing behaviors."[42]
- ◆ "The structural disconnect of youth from adults may generate in at least some youth a hunger for meaningful relationships with mature adults. For many youth do in fact desire the boundaries, teaching, direction, wisdom, and caring that adults can offer."[43]
- ◆ "Children benefit enormously from being around caring people in all stages of the life cycle. They benefit in special ways from being around old people, including, of course, their grandparents."[44]
- ◆ "To be healthy and able to succeed, each child . . . needs a significant relationship with at least three adults besides her or his parents."[45]

Parents who believe their children need the influence of adults outside the home can just cross their fingers and hope for the best.

Or parents can take the initiative to ensure their children and teenagers form kingdom relationships.

"Who are the powerful, compelling examples of a life of faith your children see day in and day out? Young people aren't necessarily looking for 'cool' Christians, but they are looking for authentic Christians, those whose bold actions match their challenging words. Find men and women who love God passionately and invite them to your home. Let your children hear their stories, and let them be infected with their passionate desire to know and serve God."[46]

Parents who make church life a high priority for their families have the greatest opportunity to expose their children to kingdom adults.

- ◆ Children and teenagers who attend regularly are likely to form relationships with adults who carry impact.
- ◆ Children and teenagers who attend sporadically seldom establish relationships with adults that matter.

Wise parents invite into their homes the ministers and key leaders from church who impact their children. They create an opportunity for their children to bond with their leaders in a way that would be difficult at church.

Support for Church Leaders

Wise parents do not speak critically about ministers and church leaders in the presence of their children. Such conversations can permanently damage the relationship between children and their leaders and thus negate spiritual impact.

Wise parents do not negate the teaching church leaders have done with their children unless a serious biblical error has been made. In general, parents should take a biblical stance when questions arise rather than joining their child in criticizing the leader. For instance, consider the following scenario.

Jill comes home from a True Love Waits weekend looking a little upset. Mom asks Jill what's bothering her, and Jill says that one of the subjects discussed over the weekend was modest dress. Jill remarks, "According to what they said, I shouldn't be wearing half the clothes I own. I don't like anyone telling me how I should dress."

Mom can make one of two responses here.

She can say, "Honey, I think you look just fine. Sometimes those people at the church just get a little unreasonable. Besides, you're just wearing what's in style. You're not doing anything wrong."

Or she can respond in this way: "Let's take some time to consider what the Bible teaches in regard to modesty and purity. Then we can decide together if you need to make some wardrobe changes."

Parents who quickly write off the biblical teachings of church leaders as being "too radical" or "legalistic" or "just the minister's opinion" may undermine the authority of Scripture in their child's life.

◆ Parents should keep the family centered on the church to expose their children to godly adults.

◆ Parents should be thankful when other adults invest in their children.

◆ Parents equally should feel motivated to make a kingdom impact in the lives of the kids of others.

Parents Investing in Other Children

Kingdom parents can make an eternal impact in the lives of children from other homes.

RESEARCH CONCLUSION

Parents should make better efforts to learn teens' names, to strike up conversations with teens, to ask meaningful questions of youth, to be vulnerable themselves to youth in various ways, to show some interest in teens, to help connect them to jobs and internships, to make themselves available in times of trouble and crisis, to work toward becoming models and partners in love and concern and sacrifice. . . . None of this takes a Master of Divinity degree. It is simply a matter of appreciation, attention, effort, and continuity from ordinary mature adults.[47]

1. Kingdom parents can present the gospel to lost children and teenagers. Some parents say their home feels like Grand Central Station with children coming and going. Alert parents will watch for opportunities for conversations with some of those children that can turn toward salvation.

2. Kingdom parents informally can share truth with those who come under their roof.

3. Kingdom parents can allow the Christian atmosphere of their homes to make a lifetime impression on those who never see such a model. They can become intentional about letting others observe truth lived out in home relationships.

4. Kingdom parents can help fill the emotional emptiness of children and teenagers who receive little love, affirmation, or focused attention in their own homes.

5. Kingdom parents can become prayer warriors for the children who come to their homes, in some cases becoming the only people who are bringing a child's name before God.

Kingdom parents need to see their home as their primary mission field.

SUMMARY

♦ Relationships are central to making a kingdom impact on children.

♦ Children and even teenagers want genuine relationships with adults.

♦ It is not the arrival of adolescence that produces problems within children. Those who do develop problems usually are just reflecting the fact that all is not well around them.

- Children and teenagers need parents and other adults in their lives who have a genuine, vibrant relationship with Jesus Christ. They will grow up to be much like them.

- Many children reared in spiritually shallow homes become spiritually shallow young adults. Others walk away from the faith altogether.

- Parents who are clueless related to how their own personalities are impacting their children are destined to weak parenting.

- Children and teenagers tend to embrace the faith of parents who have heart connections with their offspring.

- Children and teenagers tend to embrace the faith of parents who show them unfailing love in ways they can understand.

- Children and teenagers tend to embrace the faith of parents who have a healthy, biblical view of self.

- Children and teenagers tend to embrace the faith of parents who maintain open communication with them.

- Children and teenagers tend to embrace the faith of parents who communicate their significance and provide encouragement.

- Children and teenagers tend to embrace the faith of parents who spend focused time with them.

- Children and teenagers tend to embrace the faith of parents in a vibrant, lifetime marriage.

- Children and teenagers tend to embrace the faith of parents who relate to them with grace.

- Adult relationships outside the family can have a kingdom impact on children and youth.

- Parents who make church life a high priority for their families have the greatest opportunity to expose their children to kingdom adults.

- Kingdom parents can make an eternal impact on the lives of children from other homes.

CHAPTER 7

IMPACTING CHILDREN AND TEENAGERS AT HOME

SPIRITUAL INSTRUCTION IN THE HOME always has been God's ideal.

"These words that I am giving you today are to be in your heart. Repeat them to your children. Talk about them when you sit in your house and when you walk along the road, when you lie down and when you get up" (Deut. 6:6–7).

> He commanded our fathers,
> That they should make them known to their children;
> That the generation to come might know them,
> The children who would be born,
> That they may arise and declare to their children,
> That they may set their hope in God,
> And not forget the works of God,
> But keep His commandments
> (Ps. 78:4–7 NKJV).

"Teach a youth about the way he should go; even when he is old he will not depart from it" (Prov. 22:6).

"And fathers, don't stir up anger in your children, but bring them up in the training and instruction of the Lord" (Eph. 6:4).

Parents who want to see their children become kingdom young adults:

- ◆ Have a deep appreciation for ministers and church leaders who impact their children.
- ◆ Work aggressively to deepen relationships between their children and those church leaders.
- ◆ Build family schedules around the ministries and services of the church.
- ◆ Become firm supporters of all the church is doing to impact their children spiritually.

But at the same time parents never abdicate to the church the final responsibility for the spiritual instruction of their children and teenagers.

FACT

"Parents are the primary Christian educators in the church, and the family is the God-ordained institution for building faith in young people and for passing faith on from one generation to the next."[1]

CHILDREN AND TEENAGERS ARE TEACHABLE AT HOME

Despite their instinctive individualism, children and even teenagers are eminently teachable at home.

Josh McDowell said, "Young people say their number one source of spiritual truth is Mom and Dad—not the church, not the youth pastor or anyone else."[2]

RESEARCH CONCLUSION

"A major study revealed that while youth go to each other first for advice, they tend not to trust the advice they receive. The youth surveyed said overwhelmingly that they would prefer to go to their parents or other adults first, but they do not believe they have a relationship with them that allows them to talk openly about their problems."[3]

TOO FEW PARENTS PROVIDE SPIRITUAL INSTRUCTION

When it comes to many things (school, sports, other extracurricular activities), parents give direct instruction, but when it comes to things of the faith, parents sometimes abdicate to the church.

RESEARCH CONCLUSIONS

- "Only 10 percent of church families discusses its faith with any degree of regularity; in 43 percent of the homes . . . faith is never discussed."[4]
- "When asked how often they have devotions or worship as a family, 64 percent reported that their family rarely or never did so. Only 9 percent reported holding family devotions with any degree of regularity."[5]

On the other hand, here is the good news.

- "Religious practices in the home virtually *double* the probability of a congregation's youth entering into the life and mission of Christ's church."[6]

Of course, kingdom parents don't need research to convince them that spiritual leadership in the home is vital.

- They honor God in their home because he is the sovereign Lord of the universe.
- They joyfully accept his authority because they revere him, love him, and have hearts of gratitude toward him.

- They embrace his principles of parenting and family life because he is God and because they know his precepts offer the only hope for a healthy family.
- They assume their rightful place as spiritual leaders in the lives of their children as an expression of obedience to God.

THE POWER OF PRAYER

Spiritual instruction and impact in the home lacks power without prayer.

Bruce Wilkinson has observed:

- "The sobering news about raising children is that we really have no ultimate control over whether our child will choose the narrow gate 'that leads to life' (Matthew 7:14 NIV) or the wide gate that leads to destruction. If other experiences in life have not humbled us and shown us how dependent we are on God, then parenting a preadolescent or teenager will.
- "But understanding our desperate need to depend on God is the good news. Once we give up the naïve idea that we parents can dictate the choices our children will make and the spiritual gate—narrow or broad—they will walk through, then we are ready to slip on the knee pads and get serious about prayer."[7]

Most of the prayers parents will pray over their children will be closet prayers. Some concerns only can be expressed in private. But the compliment to closet prayers are those prayers children get to hear.

- Children and teenagers must hear kingdom parents crying to God for them.
- They need to hear the depth of their parents' love revealed in those prayers.

- ◆ They need to hear how keenly their parents want to see impact radiating out from their lives.
- ◆ They need to hear their parents release them to God's call and purposes.

Hearing such prayers may be one of the most important experiences a child can have.

For many years I have used a daily plan for praying over my son Clayton. It brings variety to my prayers each morning, and it keeps me from forgetting issues to pray about. This prayer plan can be found at the end of this chapter. Regardless of the plan or approach, parents need to cry out to God for each of their children each morning.

INFORMAL SPIRITUAL INSTRUCTION AT HOME

"These words that I am giving you today are to be in your heart. Repeat them to your children. Talk about them when you sit in your house and when you walk along the road, when you lie down and when you get up" (Deut. 6:6–7).

Kingdom parents provide spiritual instruction in the home both formally and informally. "When you sit in your house" sounds like formal instruction, something that is planned and prepared for. "When you walk by the way" sounds less formal and even spontaneous. Both are vital.

1. Informal spiritual impact can take place without words.
- ◆ "When a congenial relationship exists between parents and their children, the youth tend to adopt their parents' values even though they are never discussed directly."[8]

2. Informal spiritual impact also takes place as kingdom parents model truth and values.
- ◆ "These values-in-action of the parents are the ones that children see and imitate. For this reason parents who intend to

communicate traditional moral values to their children need to be conscious of how they, as parents, live, speak, and behave."[9]

♦ Parents who use the narcotic ethyl (beverage) alcohol negate instruction they intend to give on other drugs.

♦ Parents who fudge on income taxes negate instruction they intend to give on cheating in school.

♦ Parents who speed when driving negate instruction they intend to give on respect for the rule of law.

♦ Parents who ask children to tell phone callers they are not home negate instruction they intend to give on honesty.

3. Informal spiritual impact also takes place as parents use gentle reasoning to communicate values.

♦ "Studies show that youth are more likely to internalize traditional values if an adult uses discussion to explain why certain moral laws are important, and that breaking them can violate one's own inner needs as well as bring unhappiness to someone else."[10]

FORMAL SPIRITUAL INSTRUCTION IN THE HOME

"He said to them, 'Take to heart all these words I am giving as a warning to you today, so that you may command your children to carefully follow all the words of this law'" (Deut. 32:46).

Informal spiritual instruction in the home is vital but can never take the place of intentional times the family gathers to talk of the things of God.

Studying the Bible as Families

Henry Blackaby notes, "Each parent must teach God's Word to their children out of their own heart, with all diligence. We are not to teach them casually or carelessly or occasionally, but diligently.

Our children must recognize that God's Word is vital in our lives and, therefore, is to be vital in their own."[11]

God-Centered Worldview

Parents must use family Bible study time to assist their children in forming a God-centered worldview. "Another term for worldview is a philosophy of life. We define worldview as the underlying belief system held by an individual that determines his/her attitudes and actions about life."[12] Every person has such a belief system.

The following three statements could not be more central to parenting.

- "A person's concept of reality and truth determines his beliefs!
- A person's beliefs shape his values!
- A person's values drive his actions!"[13]

Because of the decay of American culture, the God-centered worldview children need to construct:

- Will be at odds with the views of many of their peers.
- May be at odds with the educational system they are part of.
- Will certainly be at odds with the entertainment industry that intrudes into their lives.

Parents can be grateful for any assistance the church is giving in teaching a God-centered worldview to their children. But at the same time, parents cannot abdicate to the church the final responsibility for ensuring this is done.

Parents need to ask themselves:

- To what degree does each of my children see the world and make decisions based on the supremacy of the Lord Jesus Christ?
- To what degree does each of my children see the world and make decisions based on his or her desire to see God's kingdom come on earth?

- To what degree does each of my children see the world and make decisions based on a desire to embody God's name, reflect his character, and obey his word?
- To what degree does each of my children see the world and make decisions from the perspective of eternity?

Absolute Truth

Parents must teach the Bible to their children in a way that affirms Scripture as absolute truth. Powerful voices consistently tell children and teenagers that:

- All truth is relative.
- Being sincere is more important than being right.
- Respecting others means accepting whatever they believe as the truth.
- There are many ways to know God, and they all are equally valid.

Most children and teenagers believe God exists to make them happy and solve their problems. They increasingly see Jesus as a little friend in their pocket whom they can take out when they have a problem to solve. Few children or teenagers are grasping that they exist for the glory of God.

Most children and teenagers cannot put their beliefs into words. They have only hazy concepts of the most basic Christian beliefs.

Parents are in a battle for the hearts and minds of their children. The voices that would confuse their kids are loud and often have hours a week to communicate their messages. In the best of situations, parents have too few minutes to confront those voices. Therefore, parents must not ever allow busy schedules to keep them from gathering the family for warm, Spirit-empowered Bible teaching.

Printed Guide

Parents need a guide to know how best to move through Scripture over the years. They also profit from printed guidance in knowing how to make timeless truths come alive for a new generation. Church leaders need to place in the hands of parents publications that provide a plan for family study and worship.

Parents need a printed plan that:

- ◆ Has an overarching plan to present the full counsel of Scripture over a period of time.
- ◆ Has creative approaches that make teaching relevant and interesting to specific ages of children.
- ◆ Has creative ways to make family worship warm, intimate, and relational.
- ◆ Has a variety of ways for families to pray together.

Practicing Spiritual Disciplines as Families

Parents must lead their children to practice spiritual disciplines such as Scripture memory and prayer.

RESEARCH CONCLUSION

"[Children] should also be taught to practice their faith in the sense of consistently working on skills, habits, and virtues in the direction of excellence in faith, analogous to musicians and athletes practicing their skills. Many religious teens in the US appear to engage in few religious practices. But even basic practices like regular Bible reading and personal prayer seem clearly associated with stronger and deeper faith commitment among youth."[14]

Sharing Testimonies

Parents must create opportunities for family members to share spiritual testimonies.

Tom Elliff reminds parents: "One day it will be impossible for your friends and family members to access all that is stored up in the library of your heart. That is why it is imperative for you to share with them now the simple story of your conversion. A legacy of faith in Christ is the most important thing you can leave with them. So, tell them 'your story.' And, while you're at it, ask them about theirs."[15]

Beyond their story of conversion, parents need to tell their children what God has been teaching them lately. They need to describe ways they are growing in the Christian life.

QUESTION

How many days, months, or years has it been since you said things like this to your child?

- ◆ "Come sit down over here. I want to share with you something new that God is doing in my life right now?"
- ◆ "I have been looking forward to breakfast this morning because I want to tell you what God showed me in Scripture during my quiet time early this morning?"
- ◆ "The truth of that sermon hit me hard this morning. Son, you need to know what I committed to God at the close of the service?"

They need to explain how they have made moral decisions and life decisions recently.

- ◆ "Son, in this crazy world I probably could figure out some way to have an affair. But I never have and never will. Can I share with you why I am absolutely faithful to your mother?"
- ◆ "Sweetheart, come over here and look at this income tax form. I want to show you a box where I could fudge on a number and never be caught. Can I explain to you why I choose to be completely honest with my taxes?"

Parents' past and present testimony will shape a kingdom generation. The absence of such words will stunt the next generation.

Praying as Families

Family prayer must be a part of formal spiritual instruction. Prayer during family worship and devotionals will seem more natural if parents pray with their children every night. Praying with toddlers at bedtime seems comfortable to most Christian parents, but seventeen-year-olds need it just as much (and perhaps more).

Prayer during family times must have variety. Too much predictable sameness makes prayer seem like a ritual. Parents and even children need to think of new ways to pray, new places to pray, and new words in prayer.

Family prayers should include prayer for one another. Parents may find it meaningful to stand behind children with hands on their shoulders or head while they pray over them. Children can do the same over parents and siblings.

As with any prayer group, families should be faithful in recording their prayers of intercession so later they can record the ways God chose to answer. Such journaling teaches children a life-altering lesson about the power of prayer.

Starting New Traditions for the Family

Mark Matlock speaks to tens of thousands of teenagers a year, but he knows the power of parents to impact their lives. "Some of us experienced wonderful parents who instilled in us a sense of destiny in following God's wonderful plan for our lives, but for others, the task is not to extend a positive family legacy, but to begin one. Starting today, every Christian parent can begin to create an environment of hope, vision, and excitement about following the greatest Leader the world has ever known in the greatest challenge we can ever experience."[16]

DISCIPLINE IN THE HOME

In some homes adult self-fulfillment and stress avoidance take precedence over the demanding work of disciplining children. Children with a kingdom focus seldom come from homes with weak discipline.

"My son, keep your father's command, and don't reject your mother's teaching" (Prov. 6:20).

"A rod of correction imparts wisdom, but a youth left to himself is a disgrace to his mother" (Prov. 29:15).

Bruce Wilkinson says to parents:

♦ "As a parent you have authority because God calls you to be an authority in your child's life.

♦ You have the authority to act on behalf of God.

♦ As a father or mother, you do not exercise rule over your own jurisdiction but over God's.

♦ You act at His command.

♦ You discharge a duty that He has given.

♦ You may not try to shape the lives of your children as pleases you but as pleases Him."[17]

James Dobson adds:

♦ "I am recommending a simple principle: when you are defiantly challenged, win decisively.

♦ When the child asks, 'Who's in charge?' tell him.

♦ When he mutters, 'Who loves me?' take him in your arms and surround him with affection.

♦ Treat him with respect and dignity, and expect the same from him.

♦ Then begin to enjoy the sweet benefits of competent parenthood."[18]

Modeling God's justice means parents are in authority over their children. They make decisions about structure, limits, and behavior;

and they enforce those decisions. They never stop parenting, even when they are emotionally tired.

When older children and teens pull against their decisions and their structure, they hold the rope. They dole out more rope as kids show growing maturity and responsibility, but they never turn loose completely.

Here is a paradox:

◆ The parent who chooses to be a buddy instead of a parent likely will not end up with a buddy but with an estranged teenager or young adult. On top of that, parents who try to be buddies seldom rear children with a kingdom focus.

◆ The parent who chooses to be a parent instead of a buddy likely will end up with a warm, lifetime friendship with that child. On top of that, godly parents who parent are most likely to rear kingdom kids.

Modeling Obedience and Submission to God

Children who watch their parents graciously and positively live in submission to God's authority are not likely to conclude that those same parents lord it over them for their own ego needs. Those kids intuitively seem to know it is safe to obey someone who himself has chosen to live under authority.

A Roman centurion came to see Jesus. The soldier was both under the authority of his commanders and exercised authority over his subordinates. This helped him clearly to see his need to come under the ultimate authority of Jesus. The soldier's clear understanding of spiritual authority and relationships caused Jesus to remark, "I tell you, I have never found anyone in Israel with faith like this" (Matt. 8:10 TEV). Children and teenagers are likely to follow a parent who honors God's authority.

Using Consequences to Discipline

"Discipline your son while there is hope; don't be intent on killing him" (Prov. 19:18).

Many parents respond to disobedience with emotional outbursts. Usually those are weak responses with limited impact. "A gentle answer turns away anger, but a harsh word stirs up wrath" (Prov. 15:1).

Yelling

+ Is a choice. No child can make a parent yell.
+ Is a sign of an emotional weakness in the parent.
+ Usually mimics the yelling a parent's parent practiced.
+ Frightens children when supposedly strong parents lose emotional control.
+ Damages a child's sense of self.
+ Pushes children away.
+ Leads to injuries that can last for years.
+ Makes restoring closeness later much more difficult.
+ Seldom leads a child or teenager to a permanent change of heart.
+ Leads children to become cold, distant teenagers.

Parents who want kingdom kids to emerge from their homes will stop using emotional outbursts as their typical response to bad behavior. Connecting behavior with consequences is far more effective than sharp words in changing the bad behavior.

Kingdom parents let their children know what the limits are.

+ "You may play anywhere in our yard, but you may not leave our yard."
+ "You may choose any game you want that does not exceed the rating limit we have set."

- ◆ "You may not stay out a minute later than the curfew we have set for you."

Natural Consequences

When children and youth disobey, they need to experience the natural consequences of their actions. Natural consequences are outcomes kids experience on their own without the intervention of parents. A child who disobeys about completing studies and then is suspended from a sports team over grades is experiencing natural consequences.

Wise parents do not step in to rescue their kids from the natural consequences of their actions. With rare exceptions they allow those consequences to become powerful teachers for the future.

At times, however, natural consequences are inadequate in themselves to decrease foolishness because they lack power or they come too late.

Logical Consequences

When natural consequences are insufficient to confront a rebellious child's behavior, wise parents engineer logical consequences. Logical consequences are both intense and immediate.

Placing a child in time out, grounding a child, and taking away car keys are all logical consequences. They are not a natural result of disobedience but are a response parents have engineered. They allow a child quickly to see the foolishness of his choices.

Good Behavior

Parents need to show children every time their good choices lead to positive, natural consequences. And parents need to create positive, logical consequences (rewards) in response to other good choices. Highlighting positives is just as important as giving attention to negative consequences.

Mutual Accountability When Appropriate

As my own son approached adolescence, I had to decide whether to mimic the majority of parents I had observed during three decades as a youth minister. I had observed most parents in a cat-and-mouse game related to issues of morality. Here were the suppositions underlying the game:

1. Parents have their act together, but teenage children are always pulled toward the dark side of life.
2. Teenagers typically hide their darker leanings from parents through clever deception.
3. Parents must use skill and daily vigilance to catch their teenagers in those deceptions.

Two thoughts kept me from beginning the same game with my own son.

1. I was keenly aware that my fallen nature is just as problematic as his. I needed accountability just as much as he.
2. I guessed that he would welcome mutual accountability but would find six years of playing cops and robbers distasteful.

In a quieter moment, I said to my son: "Clayton, what you least need these days is a dad who experiences a moral failure. Not only would this offend God, but it would harm your life in many ways. And naturally a moral failure in your life would break my heart as well. Since we already have our hearts connected and trust each other, how about we gently hold each other accountable in areas of morality and purity?"

Clayton responded warmly and positively, a vastly different reaction than I have seen in some homes. We have developed questions we ask each other related to thoughts and actions over the past week. Since I am just as responsible for answering the questions as my son, this time never feels like the third degree. Many families might choose gentle, grace-filled accountability over an alternative that seldom is effective.

Vigilance with the Media

God expects parents to serve as the gatekeepers who decide which voices and influences enter their homes.

- ◆ Kingdom parents study rating systems for games, music, and media and stand firm on what may enter their home. Other parents don't raise the issue because they fear making their children unhappy.
- ◆ Kingdom parents designate acceptable television programs that build children rather than harm them. Other parents let the television run all day with no thought of the impact.
- ◆ Kingdom parents study Christian reviews of movies before sending their kids there. Other parents don't want arguments so they keep quiet.
- ◆ Kingdom parents disable Internet access when no parent will be home. Other parents hope some inadequate filter will provide a little protection while they are gone.

In the real world what parents do about the media matters.

- ◆ Children who have spent hundreds of hours splattering video opponents with shotguns may find kingdom compassion for others difficult some day.
- ◆ Children who have spent hundreds of hours repeating the despondent lyrics of music may find kingdom optimism hard to embrace some day.
- ◆ Children who have spent hundreds of hours looking at images of naked people in every kind of perversion may find kingdom purity elusive some day.
- ◆ Children who have spent hundreds of hours listening to the mesmerizing messages of nonstop television may find a kingdom worldview unacceptable some day.

An executive with a twenty-four-hour music/television network once said: "We don't influence your teenager. We own your teenager." Kingdom parents must decide if this will be true.

CLINICAL OBSERVATION

"When parents are very emotionally warm, available, and affectionate and balance these qualities with consistently high expectations and a firm but fair disciplinary style, they create an emotional context or climate in which children thrive. Children from these homes tend to be secure, well-adjusted, and generally healthier and safer than their peers."[19]

GIVE CHILDREN AND TEENAGERS A HEART FOR THE WORLD

Begin with "Jerusalem"

A child or teenager's closest circle of friends should be growing Christians. The older children become, the more powerful the influence of that inner circle becomes. This same principle applies to teenagers they date or court. They must be maturing Christians, or harm usually will follow.

Parents who desire to rear kingdom children will lead them first to have a heart for lost people near at hand. Christian kids in firm relationships with an inner circle of other Christians can safely reach out to lost peers. In essence those Christian friends become a rescue squad holding on to and supporting one another as they reach across the quicksand to friends who need Jesus.

Some church parents, fearful of the world, try to isolate their children from the lost. Those same parents probably hope their children will grow up to be strong adults who then will try to win the world to Jesus. Unfortunately, there is no magic switch a parent can throw to change an older teen's mind-set from "avoid lost people at all costs" to "redeem all persons to Christ." Parents who have reared the family with a bunker mentality probably will get young adults content to live out their lives in that bunker.

On the other hand, children who can't remember a time when family members weren't focused on lost friends and acquaintances will probably grow into a young adult with a heart for the world. A heart for his "Jerusalem" will easily lead to a concern for the "uttermost parts of the earth."

QUESTIONS

- How many days or years has it been since you joined with your child to pray by name for a lost friend?
- Which acquaintance of your child could you volunteer to help your child pick up for church this Sunday or Wednesday?
- Could your children name an adult friend of yours they know you are seeking to lead to Christ?
- When was the last time someone made a profession of faith that a member of your family had a part in reaching?
- What step can you take this week to lead members of your family to have hearts for the lost?

Family Missions Service

Parents who perform acts of missions and service with their children make a lifetime impact on those children.

RESEARCH CONCLUSION

"[Children's] memories of involvement in service are better predictors of their faith maturity as adults than their memories of participation in Sunday school, Bible study, or worship services."[20]

This research from Search Institute does not suggest that church Bible study and worship are unimportant. They are foundational for any Bible-believing family. The research does suggest, though, that most kingdom-focused young adults tend to have experienced missions and service while young. Parents who never do such activities with their children or teenagers are missing one of their most powerful opportunities for impact.

God calls families to missions locally, nationally, and globally. Parents need to partner with church leaders to become knowledgeable about opportunities for families in each arena.

Gary Smalley notes: "Taking mini-mission trips to your local Salvation Army to serve Thanksgiving dinner or help the poor can be a tremendous bonding time, or plan several years in advance to save up to visit one of your church's missionaries in the field. . . . [You will] never lose the closeness that can come from trips like these."[21]

Family Finances

Family mission trips nationally and globally require money. God may be calling families to choose to live more frugally than necessary in order to release unusual funds for kingdom expansion. Some years an international mission trip as a family may take priority over the newest high-definition big screen television.

Wise parents involve children and teenagers in making decisions about finances. A family meeting might include questions such as:

- ◆ Since our family has more than enough resources, how much do each of you suggest we commit to ministry with starving people each month?
- ◆ Who would be willing to do a Web search of organizations that assist starving people in the name of Jesus Christ?
- ◆ What can each of you suggest we cut back on so we will have enough money to commit to this project each month?

◆ How can we get stories and feedback from the organization
we channel our gifts through so we can know of the kingdom
impact being made?

Family Prayer for the World

Children who have grown up praying about global kingdom issues are most likely to become kingdom-focused young adults. Wise
parents will include prayer for the nations and for kingdom concerns
when the family gathers for study and worship. Parents can ask
church leaders to help them find printed and Internet sources for
fresh prayer needs, locally and globally.

International Relationships

Children and teenagers will sense a closer bond with a region of
the world when they have developed relationships with persons
there. Family or church mission trips to a new region provide the
most powerful new relationships. A trip taken during childhood
might cause such a bond with a people group that a grown child
might make trips back for a lifetime.

Parents can also nurture global relationships by orchestrating
their children meeting internationals living in the US. A child
might always feel closeness with a country or people group repre-
sented by an engaging international student invited to share
Thanksgiving with the family.

TELEVISION

Church parents sometimes say:
◆ I know we should be praying and studying as Christian
families, but honestly we can't find even fifteen minutes for
such gatherings.

◆ I know doing a service project as a family would be memorable, but where in our feverish schedule would that ever fit?

◆ I know I need to go to my kids' bedrooms more often for long
talks, but all I have time for is just the basics to keep our
home operating.

Somehow the math does not add up. The average adult watches
television two hours and thirty-eight minutes per day. Perhaps parents have more discretionary time than they realize. If parents
watched one hour of television an evening, suddenly ninety-eight
minutes would be available for family worship, supervising homework projects, crafting wise discipline, and listening to the hearts of
children or teens.

Church families will not reach their potential as kingdom families until they begin to manage television.

CHALLENGES

1. Turn off the television during meals. Families that watch
television instead of enjoying conversation during mealtime are dys-
functional. They are using media to anesthetize their lack of communication. Parents who want healthy, kingdom kids will turn the
set off.

2. Turn on the set only for specific programs. The television
and the microwave are appliances, and they should be on only when
it serves a purpose. Televisions that stay on hours at a time have
enormous power to impact children, teenagers, and even adults. Sets
that stay on for hours add to the noise and chaos of the home. Sets
that stay on for hours hypnotically catch the attention of family
members who otherwise would do something purposeful.

**3. Turn on the set primarily for programs to be viewed as a
family.** Watching television together allows at least some opportunity
for communication and closeness. Watching television together
allows parents to raise issues related to worldview and values being

communicated. Watching television together means the set can be off before and after the program the family has chosen for the evening.

4. Apply the same standards of morality to the programs you watch as to guests in your home. Do you allow guests in your home to curse in front of your children? Do you allow unmarried persons to sleep together in your guest room? Do you allow guests to get drunk in your family room? Do you allow guests to become violent in front of your children? Why would you have a double standard? Why would you believe powerful television images are less a moral issue than persons in your home?

5. Avoid placing television sets in children's bedrooms. Such an error guarantees a major loss of communication in families. One of the few values of owning a television is the power it has to draw the family together to the family room. This value is lost if family members separate for hours to their separate sets. Such separation becomes even more damaging when teenagers have the option of spending long hours alone in their rooms with a private TV. (Parents who dread pulling sets out of bedrooms need to consider whether their goal is to be a buddy or a parent to their children.)

6. Carefully evaluate whether to place a set in the master bedroom. Parents need to consider whether they want a set in order to watch programs "not suitable for the kids." Is immorality more acceptable for adults than for the young? Will children be confused by parents who speak against sinful thoughts and deeds but seem to enjoy watching that in others? Parents also need to consider whether a set in the master bedroom represents an escape from active parenting. With so few minutes between dinner cleanup and bedtime, parents must evaluate carefully the temptation to escape into a hypnotic trance rather than connecting with the children.

7. Consider buying a digital video recorder. Parents need to lead the family to decide how much television to watch, what to watch, and when to watch. Those are complicated decisions.

What and when the family chooses to watch almost never will correspond with broadcast schedules. Busy families need an easy way to record those rare programs appropriate for Christians so they can be viewed at the precise time that best fits the family schedule. Also, gathering the family for a meal or for prayer becomes less traumatic when programs airing then can be recorded for later.

8. Make a firm decision when the television will be turned off for the night. That time should allow preparation for bed without chaos. That time should allow parents to end the day with relaxed conversation and prayer with children. That time should allow parents and children to get the sleep recommended for their age groups.

Taming the television can mark a major step toward becoming a kingdom family.

PARTNERING WITH THE CHURCH FOR GREATER IMPACT AT HOME

Many church parents experience shock and awe when they discover they are to be the primary spiritual leaders to their children. Most assume that duty lies with church ministers and leaders. It doesn't.

Parents ready to assume this amazing responsibility need all the help and support they can get. Though church ministers and leaders are not the primary spiritual leaders of children, they can be powerful partners with parents ready to take on this role.

Training in Parenting

Parents of infants and parents of college students need specific training in parenting. As children grow, parents find themselves parenting every age of child for the first time. Without specific training, most parents tend to reproduce the failed parenting approaches their own parents may have used. Parents need to partner with church leaders in designing training events that provide instruction in both parenting and spiritual leadership.

Most church leaders already are overworked and under resourced. It is unfair for parents to ask for new attention to home issues without offering their time, support, and resources for these new ministry ventures.

A partnership between parents and church leaders offers the greatest opportunity to grow children into kingdom young adults.

SUMMARY

- ◆ Spiritual instruction in the home always has been God's ideal.
- ◆ Parents never abdicate to the church the final responsibility for the spiritual instruction of their children and teenagers.
- ◆ Children and even teenagers are eminently teachable at home.
- ◆ Spiritual instruction and impact in the home lacks power without prayer.
- ◆ Kingdom parents provide spiritual instruction in the home both formally and informally.
- ◆ Informal spiritual impact takes place as kingdom parents model truth and values.
- ◆ Informal spiritual impact takes place as parents use gentle reasoning to communicate values.
- ◆ Kingdom parents must teach God's Word to their children out of their own hearts.
- ◆ Kingdom parents must lead their children to practice the spiritual disciplines.
- ◆ Kingdom parents must create opportunities for family members to share spiritual testimonies.
- ◆ Kingdom parents must make family prayer a part of formal spiritual instruction.

- ◆ Children with a kingdom focus seldom come from homes with weak discipline.
- ◆ Children and teenagers know it is safe to obey a parent who himself has chosen to live under God's authority.
- ◆ Connecting behavior with consequences is far more effective than sharp words in changing behavior.
- ◆ Parents who perform acts of missions and service with their children make a lifetime impact on those children.
- ◆ Taming the television can mark a major step toward becoming a kingdom family.
- ◆ A partnership between parents and church leaders offers the greatest opportunity to grow children into kingdom young adults.

Parents' Prayers

Each of the numbers below represent a day of the month. Parents can pray over their children a unique way each of thirty days each month. Some parents place this list in their personal digital accessory to make it more available each morning.

❖ ❖ ❖

Day 1—Salvation
Lord, let salvation spring up within my children that they may obtain the salvation that is in Christ Jesus, with eternal glory (Isa. 45:8; 2 Tim. 2:10).

Day 2—Growth in Grace
I pray that they may "grow in the grace and knowledge of our Lord and Savior Jesus Christ" (2 Pet. 3:18).

Day 3—Love
Grant, Lord, that my children may learn to live a life of love through the Spirit who dwells in them (Eph. 5:2; Gal. 5:22).

Day 4—Honesty and Integrity
May integrity and honesty be their virtue and their protection (Ps. 25:25).

Day 5—Self-control
Father, help my children not to be like many others around them, but let them be "alert and self-controlled" in all they do (1 Thess. 5:6).

Day 6—A Love for God's Word
May my children grow to find God's Word "more desirable than gold—than an abundance of pure gold; and sweeter than honey—than honey dripping from the comb" (Ps. 19:10).

Day 7—Justice
God, help my children love justice as you do and to "act justly" in all
they do (Mic. 6:8).

Day 8—Mercy
May my children always "be merciful, just as [their] Father also is
merciful" (Luke 6:36).

Day 9—Respect (for Self, Others, Authority)
Father, grant that my children may "show proper respect to everyone," as Your Word commands (1 Pet. 2:17 NIV).

Day 10—Strong, Biblical Self-esteem
Help my children develop a strong self-esteem that is rooted in the
realization that they are "God's workmanship, created in Christ
Jesus" (Eph. 2:10 NIV).

Day 11—Faithfulness
"Never let loyalty and faithfulness leave you," but bind these twin
virtues around their necks and write them on the tablet of their
hearts (Prov. 3:3).

Day 12—A Passion for God
Lord, please instill in my children a soul with a craving for you, a
heart that clings passionately to you (Ps. 63:8).

Day 13—Responsibility
Grant that my children may learn responsibility, "for each person
will have to carry his own load" (Gal. 6:5).

Day 14—Kindness
Lord, may my children "always try to be kind to each other and to
everyone else" (1 Thess. 5:15 NIV).

Day 15—Generosity

Grant that my children may "be generous, willing to share, storing up for themselves a good foundation for the age to come" (1 Tim. 6:18–19).

Day 16—Peace, Peaceability

Father, let my children "make every effort to do what leads to peace" (Rom. 14:19).

Day 17—Hope

May the God of hope grant that my children may overflow with hope and hopefulness by the power of the Holy Spirit (Rom. 15:13).

Day 18—Perseverance

Lord, teach my children perseverance in all they do, and help them especially to "run with endurance the race that lies before [them]" (Heb. 12:1).

Day 19—Humility

Lord, please cultivate in my children the ability to "show true humility toward all" (Titus 3:2).

Day 20—Compassion

Lord, please clothe my children with the virtue of compassion (Col. 3:12).

Day 21—Prayerfulness

Grant, Lord, that my children's lives may be marked by prayerfulness, that they may learn to "with every prayer and request pray at all times in the Spirit," (Eph 6:18).

Day 22—Contentment

Father, teach my children "the secret of being content in any and every situation . . . through him who gives [them] strength" (Phil. 4:12–13).

Day 23—Faith

I pray that faith will find root and grow in my children's hearts, that by faith they may gain what has been promised to them (Luke 17:5–6; Heb. 11:1–40).

Day 24—A Servant Heart

Lord, please help my children develop servant hearts, that they may serve wholeheartedly "as to the Lord and not to men" (Eph. 6:7).

Day 25—Purity

"God, create a clean heart," and let their purity of heart be shown in their actions (Ps. 51:10).

Day 26—Willingness and Ability to Work Hard

Teach my children, Lord, to value work and to work hard at everything they do, "as something done for the Lord and not for men" (Col. 3:23).

Day 27—Self-discipline

Father, I pray that my children may develop self-discipline, that they may acquire a "disciplined and prudent life, doing what is right and just and fair" (Prov. 1:3 NIV).

Day 28—Heart for Missions

Lord, please help my children to develop a heart for missions, a desire to see your glory declared among the nations, your marvelous deeds among all peoples (Ps. 96:3).

Day 29—Joy

May my children be filled "with the joy from the Holy Spirit" (1 Thess. 1:6).

Day 30—Courage

May my children always "be strong and courageous" in their character and in their actions (Deut. 31:6).

CHAPTER 8

IMPACTING CHILDREN AND TEENAGERS AT CHURCH

MANY CHURCH FAMILIES BELIEVE church is important but not too important.

RESEARCH CONCLUSIONS

- ◆ "Research suggests that religious congregations are losing out to school and the media for the time and attention of youth. . . .
- ◆ Many parents also clearly prioritize homework and sports over church or youth group attendance."[1]
- ◆ "So what place is religion able to secure among these vying institutions and activities? Quite a small place at the end of the table for a short period of time each week (if that) for most US teenagers, actually."[2]

Here is how the situation looks from the child's point of view. "In the ecology of American adolescents' lives, religion operates in a social-structurally weak position, competing for time, energy, and attention and often losing against other more dominant demands and commitments, particularly against school, television and other media. (ex: 'if I get my homework done and I don't have any sports-related activity, then I guess I will go on to youth group')."[3]

If many church families now make school and community activities higher priorities than the church, should that be a concern?

RESEARCH CONCLUSIONS

♦ "Thirty-five years of research in the church shows that the relationship of faith to daily life has changed in our culture.

♦ According to major studies conducted by Search Institute in all the largest church bodies in America, fewer church families are producing the kind of youth whose hearts are committed to the mission of Jesus Christ.

♦ The studies conclude that we are losing our youth from the church and the faith as they turn to at-risk behaviors."[4]

SPIRITUAL IMPACT ON CHILDREN AND TEENAGERS MAKES A DIFFERENCE

Kids who practice their faith and are involved at church are different.

RESEARCH CONCLUSIONS

♦ "Highly religious teenagers appear to be doing much better in life than less religious teenagers.

♦ The empirical evidence suggests that religious faith and practice themselves . . . exert significant, positive, direct and indirect influences on the lives of teenagers, helping to foster healthier, more engaged adolescents who live more constructive and promising lives."[5]

♦ "Religiosity has been found to predict academic success."[6]

- "Religious youth are less likely to associate with peers who drink or do drugs."[7]
- "Youth who never attend religious services have more than three times as many sexual partners as those who attend weekly."[8]
- "Regular (church) attendance, high importance of faith and years spent in religious youth groups are clearly associated with high self-esteem and positive self-attitudes."[9]
- "Religiously committed teenagers are more likely to volunteer in the community."[10]
- "Personal devotion among adolescents is associated with reduced risk-taking behavior. It is also associated with more effectively resolving feelings of loneliness, greater regard for the self and for others, and a stronger sense that life has meaning and purpose."[11]

Research scientist Christian Smith has found nine ways that being involved in religious life may lead to positive outcomes for children and youth.

1. Moral Directives—One's faith brings with it a sense of authority and a sense of right and wrong. Children and youth make many moral decisions on the basis of "God says so."

2. Spiritual Experiences—One's faith provides personal spiritual experiences that solidify authority from on high. Authority moves from "out there" to "inside me."

3. Role Models—One's faith brings children and teenagers into relationship with adults and peers who model and thus motivate moral living and genuine faith.

4. Community and Leadership Skills—One's faith provides opportunities for children and teenagers to observe, learn, and practice skills that are valuable both in church and in life.

5. Coping Skills—One's faith instills beliefs and practices that help children and teenagers cope with life crises in positive ways.

6. Cultural Capital—One's faith provides opportunity for broader learning about the world and about life (music and history, for example) in ways that become an advantage to children and teenagers.

7. Social Capital—One's faith provides regular opportunities for children and youth to relate to other generations in life-shaping ways.

8. Network Closure—One's faith places children and teenagers in relationships with caring adults who partner with parents in providing supervision and direction.

9. Extra-Community Links—One's faith provides children and teenagers with national and global experiences and relationships that shape life positively.[12]

KINGDOM FAMILIES MUST MAKE CHURCH LIFE A PRIORITY

The research is clear. Centering family life around the church makes a huge difference in the lives of children and teenagers. Adults who are parenting with kingdom purpose must shift family schedules and priorities in the direction of the church. The good news is, the great majority of children and teenagers will be fine with that change.

RESEARCH CONCLUSIONS

◆ "Practically all teens at every level of personal religious involvement feel quite positive about religion generally and—when they are affiliated with one—about their own religious congregations specifically."[13]

◆ "The problem is not that youth won't come to church (most will), or that they hate church (few do), or that they don't want to listen to religious ministers or mature mentoring adults (they will and do)."[14]

In the real world it all comes down to moments just like this:

Coach: "If you don't let your daughter play in the tournament Sunday morning, we will have to forfeit. Everything we have worked for this season to get here will be lost. Every girl on the team will be crushed that your family prevented them from advancing. You are making as selfish a decision as I can imagine."

Dad: "This situation is just as upsetting to me as to you. You will recall that at several organizational meetings I explained we would not support Sunday morning games. I am disappointed you did not press this issue with league leadership. I am offended that my family, my daughter, and all the other families have been put in a situation you and other leaders knew was coming. The goal of this league is to build young girls, and that is what I intend to do. I intend to let my daughter know that nothing in her life is more important on Sunday morning than worship."

Sometimes the decisions of parents need translation.

Parent: "My daughter cannot come to Sunday night youth group because a major school project due Monday must take priority."

Translation: "I stayed in the office late several days and did not pick up on this school assignment. It could have been completed before Sunday if I was on top of this."

Parent: "My son cannot go on the retreat because he cannot get off work. His boss will show no flexibility."

Translation: "When the family decided my son could take part-time employment, we parents failed to require a position that promised time off for church activities."

Parent: "As a parent who must protect the health of my daughter, I have to let her sleep in instead of joining the activity on Saturday morning."

Translation: "I have been on the computer so many evenings lately that I have failed to monitor my daughter's bedtime. Now she is showing exhaustion, and my options are limited."

Parent: "I would send my child on the mission trip, but I am frustrated the trip fee is more than what I even have in my checking account."

Translation: "I gladly paid three times as much for cheerleading camp and now have little left to support a church event."

Bottom line, in many cases it all comes down to priorities.

There is good news for parents who do choose to center life around the church. Children and youth are open to the teaching they receive there.

RESEARCH CONCLUSION

"Many youth actually consciously do want to be taught, they are open to being influenced by good word and example. Faith communities have no reason to apologize for or be insecure about teaching their youth."[15]

Parents come to the offices of counselors and church leaders when they are in crisis. Often they say, "We never thought it would come to this. How did we ever get into this situation?" The answer often is, by hundreds of decisions parents and children have made over the years.

Parents get to choose whether the church will be a priority for their families. They don't get to choose the results of that decision.

HOME AND CHURCH TEACHING ABOUT THE GLORY OF GOD

Children and teenagers are more focused on what God can do for them than what they can do for God.

RESEARCH CONCLUSIONS

- "For most US teenagers, religion is something to personally believe in which makes one feel good and resolves one's problems.
- For most, it is not an entire way of life or a disciplined practice that makes hard demands of or changes people."[16]

Children and teenagers seem to have missed the fact that they exist to bring glory to God and to bring his kingdom here on earth. Too few of them can declare: "I count everything as loss because of the surpassing worth of knowing Christ Jesus my Lord. For his sake I have suffered the loss of all things and count them as rubbish, in order that I may gain Christ" (Phil. 3:8).

Nothing matters more than rearing kingdom kids who have the glory of God as the primary motive of their lives. Mark Matlock says it this way: "The motive force in God's vision (and what is often lacking in the lives of today's generation of students) is a passion for God's glory. God's glory is the reflection of His character, His unfailing, unique attributes that make Him God. We were created to 'bear' His image, to bring Him honor and glory by living according to His vision for us. God is passionate about this, and if we understand His great love and plan for our lives, we will be passionate about it, too."[17]

Parents and church leaders must lock arms to rear a generation who live for God's glory rather than for themselves.

HOME AND CHURCH TEACHING THE BASICS OF FAITH

Children and teenagers tend to be inarticulate about their faith, their religious beliefs and practices, and its meaning or place in their lives. They have a hard time putting the basics of their faith into words.

RESEARCH CONCLUSIONS

- ◆ "We were astounded by the realization that for very many teens we interviewed, it seemed as if ours was the first time any adult had ever asked them what they believed.
- ◆ By contrast, the same teens could be remarkably articulate about other subjects about which they had been drilled, such as drinking, drugs, STDs, 'safe sex,' et cetera."[18]

Children and teenagers who cannot put their faith into words may not grasp kingdom concepts.

- ◆ Parents need to know how each child is coming along in putting faith into words.
- ◆ Parents need to assist children and teenagers at home in learning to put their faith into words.
- ◆ Parents need to provide full support to church leaders who work with children and teenagers in putting their faith into words.

Parents who have a strong desire to rear children with kingdom purposes must care about the quality of teaching and spiritual transformation that takes place at church. But they never can speak of "those people at church." There is no *they*, only *we*. Parents *are* the church. Only as parents and church leaders lock arms in a committed partnership will children and teenagers experience full transformation.

THE ROLE OF PARENTS AT CHURCH

Every Christian parent should provide concrete support to the church's ministry with their children. Some parents are called and gifted by God to be teachers to children or youth. Others are called to have ongoing ministry leadership responsibilities.

All parents who do not teach or lead weekly should provide consistent, practical ministry support.

- ◆ Parents active in planning, supporting, and sponsoring ministries with children or teenagers demonstrate to their own kids that those ministries are vital.
- ◆ Parents not active in planning, supporting, and sponsoring communicate to their own kids that those ministries are of low priority.
- ◆ Parents who participate and sponsor get to share extra time with their own children.
- ◆ Parents who never participate and sponsor are cut off from their own children during those times.

Some parents may believe in magic.

- ◆ "I so want my child to embrace the ministries and activities of the church. I feel those things will make my child a better person. But I want my child to be faithful to those activities in a way I am not willing to be. I prefer making my career and my peace of mind higher priorities. So I will just have to hope my children will ignore my example and embrace church ministries anyway."
- ◆ "I want those who minister weekly with my child at church to know how important their service is to me. But I have things I would rather do than provide support to their work. I will just have to hope they will sense my appreciation from a distance."
- ◆ "I want my child to be surrounded with godly, upright children or teenagers. I want those friends so spiritually

transformed that they make a positive impression on my child. But I have other priorities and will not assist in the ministries that could impact those children. So I will just hope my child will be magically surrounded by positive peers anyway."

Parents get to choose whether they will be vitally involved in supporting church ministries with their children. They do not get to choose the results of those choices.

INTERGENERATIONAL EXPERIENCES AT CHURCH

Parents need to provide full support for education and ministries that are targeted to specific age groups of children and youth. Parents also need to champion church experiences that bring families together. Here are several possibilities.

Family Retreats

- ◆ Dinner together by families with suggested discussion topics.
- ◆ Prayer together by families.
- ◆ Divide by sexes to answer questions and then combine to compare answers.
- ◆ One session for parents and a separate session for children or teenagers.
- ◆ Time together in father-daughter and mother-son pairs.
- ◆ Experience ropes courses or other challenges by families.
- ◆ Use a campfire service for family members to affirm one another.

Parent Appreciation Banquets

- ◆ Children or teenagers purchase tickets for parents with their own money.
- ◆ Children or teenagers prepare the food and decorate according to the theme.

- Children or teenagers wait on tables and present entertainment.

Family Fellowships

- Cookouts
- Sports, baseball, etc.
- Father-son and mother-daughter events
- Messy games
- Scavenger hunt
- Family-wed game
- Role playing, while dressed as the other generation
- "Oscars" awards show—Best Family Vacation, etc.

Family Mission Projects

- Work on homes owned by those with no resources
- Nursing home services
- Assist at a shelter (homeless, refugee resettlement, abuse)
- Backyard Bible Clubs

SUMMARY

- Many church families now make school and community activities higher priorities than the church.
- Kids who practice their faith and are involved at church are very different from their peers.
- Adults who are parenting with kingdom purpose must shift family schedules and priorities in the direction of the church.
- Parents and church leaders must lock arms to rear a generation who live for God's glory rather than for themselves.
- Parents and church leaders must lock arms to rear a generation that can articulate the basics of faith.
- Spiritual transformation and impact in the home is primary.

- Spiritual transformation in the home plus quality teaching and ministry with children and youth at church is even more powerful.
- Spiritual transformation in the home, plus quality teaching with kids at church, plus church experiences that bring families together offer the greatest probability of forming young adults with kingdom purposes.

CHAPTER 9

RELEASING CHILDREN AND TEENAGERS TO THE KINGDOM

GOD WANTS CHILDREN who embody his name, thus reflecting his character.

He wants children who obey his word.

He wants children to take his message to the nations, calling upon all peoples to align themselves with God's rule and reign.

He promises to bless kingdom children in order that all the nations of the earth might be drawn to him.

RELEASING KINGDOM CHILDREN AND TEENAGERS TO BE ON MISSION

God calls some Christians to make missions their life vocation. God calls every Christian to join him in evangelizing the world. The Great Commission is a commission to every Christian, young and old.

God calls every child, teenager, and adult to short-term missions. That fact is not debatable. The only question is, Will those he calls be obedient? A second question for families is, If children are willing to go, will their parents release them to be obedient to God?

Values of Short-term Missions Involvement

1. Obedience to sovereign God
2. Freedom from the nagging guilt that accompanies disobedience
3. Motivation for growth in the Christian disciplines
4. Deeper sensitivity to institutionalized injustice
5. Appreciation for one's blessings
6. Deeper bond with mature Christian leaders and peers
7. More humility
8. More positive attitude toward sacrifice and generosity
9. Greater affection for people of other cultures and races
10. Deeper faith from watching God do what only he can do
11. Deeper faith in the power of prayer
12. Joy from seeing lives transformed, churches established, and the kingdom expanded

When parents become kingdom persons, they rear children to see those children impact the world.

Mark Matlock says it well: "Submission to the Lordship of Christ will inspire a God-given passion to be a part of His plan for the world, and will reshape our own lives and the way we parent our children. This proper understanding of God's intention for the world enables us to give our children the 'why' behind the goals, behaviors, and values we want to instill in them."[1]

This Generation in This Generation by This Generation

Short-term missions impact those who go. Parents can celebrate that. But more importantly, those who go change the world.

Wedgwood Baptist Church in Fort Worth, Texas is a church that believes older gradeschoolers can join God in changing the world. After providing concentrated training, forth, fifth, and sixth graders lead apartment Bible clubs both locally and in other cities. Adults stay in the background while children teach the Bible, lead recreation, and share their faith one-on-one.

Teenagers and collegians can have dramatic impact as well. In some ways the youth of the world has become a people group. Through the influence of movies and television, youth worldwide are beginning to dress alike, talk alike, and see the world in similar ways.

Most of the two billion teenagers of the world are unreached. Traditional missionary strategies have been more effective in reaching children and adults. The clock is ticking. Of those youth who reach age eighteen without accepting Christ as Savior, nine of ten will spend eternity in hell.

The only viable strategy for reaching large numbers of lost youth worldwide is to mobilize Christian middle schoolers, high schoolers, and collegians to win their peers.

We must win *this generation*. They matter to God, they are central to his purposes, and they will shape the world for good or ill.

We must win *this generation in this generation*. We cannot allow millions to slip into eternity without Christ. We must win them now, before they reach adulthood.

We must win *this generation in this generation by this generation*. All Christians young and old can lead youth to Christ. But the most efficient strategy for winning them quickly and in large numbers must center on mobilizing the young to reach the young.

Calling Out Every Student to Go on an Extended Mission While Young

It is time for parents to challenge their children to spend a summer, semester, or year in full-time mission work while young.

Currently high school students typically participate in local mission projects lasting a day or summer mission trips lasting about a week. Parents know these are valuable experiences that will always have a place in ministry. At the same time the degree and depth of life transformation during such brief experiences must be somewhat limited.

A growing group of Christian leaders now are challenging *all* students to invest a summer, a semester, or a year in front-line missions service. This usually will mean going to a mission point alone or with a friend rather than with a church group. In many cases students will serve alongside career missionaries in North America or around the world. Leaders dream of a day when it will be normative for almost all to go.

Many older high school students have the maturity and the spiritual strength to serve most of the summer. High school students in such settings have proved in recent years that they can be effective in missions roles, pulling their own weight and making a kingdom impact on lost communities.

For decades we have known of the amazing ability that college students have in missions settings. Whether students choose upper high school or college for their term of service, students will accelerate the harvest worldwide.

Christian students are ready for such a broad call to missions. Their bold response to See You at the Pole, Christian equal-access clubs, peer evangelism, and True Love Waits indicates their willingness to go to the front lines. The martyrdom of some of their Christian peers has only intensified and solidified that boldness.

This generation of students understands little about denominations, missions agencies, funding plans, or administrative processes. All they know is that they have a call from God to go do something bold and kingdom-shaking. They will tend to follow any voice that promises to open those doors for them. Parents and church leaders will be most comfortable when those open doors for assignments include thorough support and supervision on the field, partnership with established career missionaries, and biblically sound doctrine.

Parents should look forward to the time when most grade schoolers will grow up already knowing they will be young missionaries some day. Such children will become high school or college students who always are listening for God to tell them it is now their time to go. Their public affirmation that the time has arrived may become one of the most common decisions at youth rallies and conferences.

Parents can enjoy dreaming about the impact of this new challenge on the church. Imagine fifteen years from now in any church when most of the deacons and Bible teachers will have clear memories of the time they spent on the front lines of missions. The spiritual climate of those churches will be completely different. In addition, returning students likely will show a lifetime willingness to join short-term mission projects nearby or away and to support missions offerings.

Placing tens of thousands of students in frontline missions roles will not increase the number of students God calls to ministry vocations. God's call is sovereign and doesn't waver. But involving students in full-time ministry for a summer or longer will dramatically increase those who will hear the call that has been there all along.

The call to be a career missionary is reserved for a few. But in this era of the church, perhaps God intends to call out most Christian students to join him full-time for a season to accelerate the harvest. That short-term missions adventure will prepare a student for a lifetime of kingdom activity.

Saving Money to Fund This Adventure

Kingdom parents need to begin Missions Adventure Savings Accounts that someday will fund their children's time of missions service. Some students will go for a summer, some a semester, and some a full year.

Ideally accounts should be opened at the birth of a child. Even couples of modest means should be able to set up an automatic draft that would move five dollars or more a month into that savings account.

In the future, church members attending baby showers might choose to make financial gifts into the Missions Adventure Savings Accounts. Similarly members and relatives might make gifts to the accounts at birthdays, graduations, and other special times. Godly grandparents might sense God's leadership to make significant gifts to each of their grandchildren's accounts along the way.

Such a plan will result in tens of thousands of students reaching upper high school or college each year with all the funds they need to invest a summer or even a year in an inner-city neighborhood or international outpost. At present, funding is a ceiling that prevents many from doing what they sense a call to do. If families save for their children, there will be no ceilings at all.

Wise parents will allow even small children to earn money that can be placed in the child's Missions Adventure Savings Accounts. When children become teenagers, they can be challenged to work as hard to save for their mission project as for a bike or car. Obviously, where a teenager's money is, his heart will be also.

Missions Adventure Savings Accounts can mean that in sixteen years we will see students ready to serve who have all the resources they need. But what about teenagers and collegians called by God to go now? If God wills for them to go now, he also will provide the resources they need.

Many parents are willing to make significant financial sacrifices to provide opportunities for their children. When the local band is invited to march in the Thanksgiving Parade on national TV, when the school French club decides to go to Paris, when a student has had a lifetime dream to go to Space Camp, parents often make the sacrifices to open those doors. Godly parents will help many students gather funds for a trip this year.

Church members may be willing to help fund a mission trip, especially if they feel comfortable with the sending organization and the way the trip will be conducted. Grandparents and other relatives also are helping to fund students who feel called to go now. Families moving in the center of God's plans will find the resources they need.

Releasing Kingdom Children to God's Care

Any discussion of releasing children to missions raises concerns for their safety. Here is an interesting question.

True or false: My teenager will be safer and better off if I dictate that he or she disobey God's will and stays close to home.

Many Christian parents have clear memories of prayers they prayed at the birth of a child. Most told God they were dedicating that child to his purposes. If fact, most affirmed that the child belonged to God and expressed gratitude for getting to rear God's child.

Parents will have to pray those same prayers again when their teenager says she feels called to serve in a high-need neighborhood or Third World country. In such a moment the protective instincts of parenting come into collision with faith in the Father.

Parents have a responsibility to ensure that their child will serve with an agency or organization that has taken every prudent measure to ensure the safety of student missionaries. Parents have a responsibility to teach their children how to minimize risks away from home.

But in the end, godly parents must place the lives of their children in the hands of the Father just as they did in the delivery room. Parents who live for the glory of God must release their children to risk and even martyrdom if sovereign God should so ordain.

RELEASING CHILDREN TO GOD'S CALL VOCATIONALLY

Some parents who have not grown into kingdom persons push their children to follow in their vocational footsteps. Here is what some may be thinking.

1. "I am happy in my vocation. I want my kids to be happy. Therefore, I want my kids to choose my vocation so they can be happy."

Consider: Before the foundation of the world, God designed your child in his mind and determined a unique plan that would bring that child meaning and purpose. At the moment of conception, that uniqueness was imprinted on your child's DNA, and nothing can alter it. The only vocation that can bring ultimate joy, meaning, and purpose to your child is the one God has ordained.

2. "I'm successful in my vocation so I am able to give my kids a head start and an advantage in this line of work."

Consider: If God did not design your child to work in your vocation, no amount of coaching, networking, or even nepotism will allow him or her to succeed. You do have gifts and abilities that can prepare your child for life and work. You need to apply the considerable strengths you have to the unique (and perhaps different) vocational direction God has selected for your child.

3. "As a midlife adult, I am feeling a need to leave a legacy once I am gone. My children carrying on my work or business can be that legacy."

Consider: Human beings arrive on earth for one reason, to advance God's kingdom by his power for his glory. Children are not to complete the mission of a parent; the parent is to complete that mission. Parents have the marvelous privilege of joining God in giving children everything they need to complete the unique mission that is theirs and theirs alone. That is the greatest legacy any parent can leave.

Releasing Kingdom Children
from Choosing "Successful" Vocations

Parents would never say these things out loud, but subconsciously these things could be affecting parents' desires for their children.

1. "I have never had much influence or power. But if I can get my child into a vocation with influence, I can begin to live vicariously through my child and prop up my own self-esteem."

Consider: Every shred of incomplete self-esteem in a parent leads to major mistakes in parenting. A parent is significant because he or she was designed in the mind of God, redeemed at great cost, granted intimacy with sovereign God, and trusted with a life mission. Nothing else matters. Once a parent is OK with himself, he is released from the need to brag to associates about the powerful or respected position his child has achieved.

2. "I have spent boatloads of money on that kid. If I can get him into something pretty lucrative, some of that cash might come back to me down the road. At least I want to be assured I never will feel any financial obligations toward my child in adulthood."

Consider: Upscale retirement centers are filled with older adults who have wealthy children, plenty of money, and expressions so sad they break your heart. The only thing that will bring joy in old age will be living dead center in God's will and watching children who are doing the same. Coins and trinkets simply will not matter.

Releasing Kingdom Children
for God's Purposes in Vocation

In the New International Version of the Bible, the familiar passage in Proverbs 22:6 reads: "Train a child in the way he should go, and when he is old he will not turn from it."

The Hebrew construction of the verse suggests that parents are to train a child in light of that child's unique personality and unique life plan. The Darby Translation of the Bible says it this way: "Train up the child according to the tenor of his way."

A Bible commentary interprets "the way" as "literally, 'his way'" Scripture calls parents to read a child according to the "bent" God has given that child.[2]

A leader who sometimes serves as a spiritual leader to the Dallas Cowboys football team once told me, "I spend the majority of the time trying to help those young dads know how to love and affirm sons in their homes who have no interest in football. I am trying to show them how to celebrate gifts in music or art or dance their sons are discovering. I'm telling you, it's tough for them."

If parents try to make children into what they cannot be, misery for both parent and child can be the only result. The alternative is to join God in discovering and then championing the unique bent he has given each one.

Parents cannot and should not try to call a son or daughter into a ministry vocation. But if that call should come, it is a joy to prepare a child for such a grand adventure.

POSSIBLE REVIVAL AND THE COMPLETED TASK

The United States deserves the judgment of God. But it is at least possible that out of his grace and mercy he will send revival instead. It is entirely his decision. Since revival is at least a possibility, it merits discussion.

Revival and Spiritual Awakening

Revival is an extraordinary movement of the Holy Spirit producing extraordinary results. God begins, at his choosing and timing, to break the hearts of those seeking him. There is a profound sense of sin, repentance, and the holiness of God. Believers confess sins openly, get right with God and others, and the church is revived. This spills over to lost people, and it cannot be controlled.

Spiritual awakening refers to a time when God transforms not only the church but also whole cultures and continents. Revivals alter the lives of individuals; awakenings alter the worldview of a whole people or culture.

There Are Signs God Is Moving in This Generation of Youth and Young Adults

Parents must take note of the fact that youth and young adults have launched most of the great revivals of history. Parents may well have the next revival generation living in their homes.

Those who have survived a lightning strike often report a tingly feeling just before it hit. An increasing number of youth leaders are having similar feelings right now. Many believe revival and sweeping awakening could come in the near future and that teenagers and collegians might be at the forefront of that movement.

Here are indications God is moving in this generation of students:

- ◆ The desire of an increasing number of students to serve on the front lines of missions while young
- ◆ The intensity with which many Christian students are worshipping
- ◆ The continuing expansion of student prayer movements, symbolized by praying around their school flag poles
- ◆ Spreading commitment to moral purity, symbolized in the international growth of the True Love Waits movement
- ◆ The zeal of an increasing number of students to take their schools for Christ

Kingdom Students May Carry the Gospel to the Last People Groups on Earth

Children, teenagers, and young adults swept up in revival quickly turn their attention to the lost. Most begin to evangelize friends and family close by. Some are mobilized to carry the gospel far away. Some receive a call to make missions their life work. Others receive a call to earn their living by secular means but to be on mission all of their lives. At times large numbers of students thrust out by revival have carried the gospel to the nations.

SECOND GREAT AWAKENING

♦ The first great wave of students propelled out by revival carried the gospel to the edges of the continents in the early 1800s.

THE GLOBAL AWAKENING

♦ The second great wave of students carried the gospel to the interiors of the continents in the early 1900s.

THE THIRD GREAT WAVE

♦ If God should choose to send revival in this day, it is possible that he will call out and launch a third great wave of students to carry the gospel to the nations. Perhaps he will raise them up to carry the gospel to the last unreached people groups on earth.

Kingdom Students May Complete the Great Commission

Parents may get to see their sons and daughters take the gospel to the last group on earth. And then, according to Scripture, the end will come.

On May 16, 2003, pastor and author John Piper presented a challenge to thirty thousand godly collegians sitting in a field in

Texas. The students stood to their feet with hands lifted to heaven as Piper gave this final challenge.

When the holiness of God is your passion, you will be
a generation who lays down your life to fill the earth with
his glory.

For the glory of God's name!

For the reward of Christ's sufferings!

In the power of God's Spirit!

For your everlasting joy!

For the vindication of God's holiness in the earth!

In the name of Jesus the Holy One of God!

Oh, be that generation! Amen.[3]

SUMMARY

- ◆ God wants children who embody his name, thus reflecting his character.
- ◆ God wants children who obey his word.
- ◆ God wants children to take his message to the nations, calling upon all peoples to align themselves with God's rule and reign.
- ◆ God calls every child, teenager, and adult to short-term missions.
- ◆ The only viable strategy for reaching large numbers of lost youth worldwide is to mobilize Christian middle schoolers, high schoolers, and collegians to win their peers.
- ◆ It is time for parents to challenge their children to spend a summer, semester, or year in full-time mission work while young.
- ◆ Kingdom parents need to begin Missions Adventure Savings Accounts that someday will fund their children's summer, semester, or year of missions service.

- Parents who live for the glory of God must release their children to risk and even martyrdom if sovereign God should so ordain.
- Parents have the marvelous privilege of joining God in giving children everything they need to complete the unique mission that is theirs alone.
- Parents may very well have the next revival generation living in their homes.
- Parents may get to see their sons and daughters take the gospel to the very last group on earth.

It is never too early to begin parenting with kingdom purpose. Nor is it ever too late.

THE PROMISES OF A KINGDOM PARENT

As you come to the end of this study, do the following promises capture the desire of your heart? Would it strengthen your resolve to move in these directions by making a formal promise to God? If we ask our teenagers to make a formal promise of purity, should parents also be willing to make concrete promises?

Either as an act of private worship or as an act of shared worship with other parents, consider using your signature below as a symbol of promises you are making to the Father.

FAMILY COVENANT

Understanding that the Christian family is at the heart of God's kingdom strategy, we join in the following covenant:

1. We will rear our children in such a manner that they will have a lifelong kingdom focus.

2. We commit to integrating God's Word into every aspect of family life through regular prayer and Bible study, through teaching and embodying holy living, and through cultivating a biblical worldview.

3. We will establish Missions Adventure Savings Accounts for each child to be involved in missions activity locally, nationally, or internationally.

4. We will prioritize Bible study and worship through our local church.

5. We will live below our means to free up abundant resources for the advance of God's kingdom.

6. We will teach family members to engage the culture by applying the salt and light of God's Word.

7. We will encourage our children to be sensitive to the Lord's call to vocational ministry.

_____

Name   Date

CELEBRATION OF A CHILD'S SALVATION AND BAPTISM

THE MOST IMPORTANT EVENT in any child's life is that time he or she receives Christ as Savior. This joyous event deserves celebration by the entire family.

Beyond the joy of celebration, a family ceremony has practical value. Most teenagers go through a period of questioning salvation experiences that happened early in life. One teenager may recall, "I remember that I made my public profession of faith the last day of Vacation Bible School. Many children went forward that same time. I wonder if I was just copying my friends. I wonder if I understood what I was doing and if I truly was saved. I wonder if I've been lost all this time."

A family celebration of a child's salvation and baptism can assist with resolving later doubts. The plans described below can preserve memories of the genuineness of this life-changing experience.

Preparations

1. Invite grandparents, extended family members, and close family friends to witness the ceremony.

2. Straighten the house. Straightening the house communicates something important is about to happen.

3. Prepare a nicer meal and use the good dishes. Such preparations let everyone know that something important is about to happen. Candlelight for both the meal and the ceremony to follow adds richness.

4. Linger at the table. There is no need to rush the evening. The ceremony itself won't last long, so savor the moment. Consider serving the meal in relaxed courses with lots of laughter and family memories mixed in.

5. Dress the way the family dresses for Sunday morning. Keep in mind you are making memories that will last a lifetime. Preparations are worth the momentary hassle.

6. Take photos. The evening likely will be one of the more special times your family will share. Parents and children will treasure photo memories.

7. Turn off every kind of phone. This is one of those rare moments that must be protected from any kind of interruption.

The Passing of the Candle

The family can provide a concrete picture of the way the gospel moves down through the generations.

The eldest grandparent present should light a candle. While holding the lighted candle, that grandparent should tell the story of how the gospel came to him or her. After telling the story of salvation, the grandparent should hand the candle to another grandparent present. As the candle is passed, each grandparent should tell the story of how the gospel came to him or her. (Grandparents too far away or too ill to be present could send their story on video.)

Next, the candle should be passed to the parents. In turn they tell their stories of how the gospel came to them. Then they should pass the candle to the eldest child who shares his or her salvation story.

After each sibling has shared, the candle should be passed to the child who just has been converted. The child at the center of the celebration should be invited to share when and how the gospel was communicated in a way that became clear. Then the child should be invited to tell about receiving Christ. Finally the child should be invited to share what Christ has meant to him or her in the days since salvation.

When the child finishes sharing, the parents should challenge that child to look forward to the day when he or she will pass both the gospel and the candle down to another generation yet unborn.

Presentation of a Bible

Parents can present to the child a keepsake Bible. One of the primary roles of this Bible will be to help preserve the memory of the salvation and baptism experiences.

The sharing the child did while holding the candle should be preserved on blank pages in the Bible. Children old enough to write their thoughts should be guided to do so. Younger children should share out loud while the parent writes the actual words of the child without editing. The testimony placed in the Bible should include thoughts leading up to salvation, memories of the moment of salvation, and early thoughts and feelings that have followed that experience. In addition to sharing thoughts and feelings about the salvation experience, the child also should be prompted to share about his or her baptism.

Parents may want to add the dates of the salvation and baptism experiences as well as the church name, senior pastor's name, and the names of any other friends or leaders who were instrumental in guiding the child toward salvation.

The testimony articulated by the child and placed in the Bible likely will be powerful in its simplicity and its sincerity. When the child becomes a teenager, he may wonder, *Did I have any idea what I was really doing?* Reading his actual thoughts and words recorded in the Bible will be powerful and may well resolve any doubts or questions that have arisen.

Because this Bible needs to last a lifetime, parents should consider providing a nice storage box.

Video

The testimonies of family members as they pass the candle down the generations will be powerful. Families can consider videoing this mountain peak moment for the child to watch again and again as the child grows up. When family members go to heaven, their video testimony becomes even more precious.

One parent can video while the other parent assists with writing the child's testimony in the Bible. The simplicity and the sincerity of the child's thoughts and memories shared aloud will complement the power of the written words.

This same video can hold footage of the child's baptism. Later footage can be added as parents ask the child to share thoughts and feelings about that baptism experience.

Mission Adventure Savings Account

If the family has a Mission Adventure Savings Account for the child, the ceremony evening would be a good time to remind the new convert about it. Parents might want to show the child a report that shows the balance of the account to date.

Family Verse

Kingdom families can consider choosing a family verse. This verse can strengthen family identity and can serve as a mission or purpose statement for the family.

The new Christian can be invited to memorize the verse and then write the verse in the keepsake Bible. Parents can point out that as a child of God the new convert can now join the family in the mission of that verse.

THE CHRISTIAN
BAR/BAT MITZVAH
AT HOME

A CHRISTIAN BAR/BAT MITZVAH can be planned for the beginning of adolescence. (*Bar* is for boys, and *bat* is for girls.) Most families will remember this ceremony for a lifetime.

For the Jewish family it means the child, at the age of thirteen, is deemed ready for religious responsibility. He or she becomes a "son/daughter of the covenant."

For the Christian youth it is a time when a young person assumes responsibility for spiritual disciplines. He begins to understand the transition that is taking place in his life as Scripture characterizes: "When I was a child, I spoke like a child, I thought like a child, I reasoned like a child. When I became a man, I put aside childish things" (1 Cor. 13:11). The Christian bar/bat mitzvah means putting away childish things and accepting the responsibility of adult spiritual disciplines. It is designed to make a significant impact on parent and child.[1]

The Date

The Christian bar mitzvah can be planned on the eve of the thirteenth birthday. Or it might be planned for the evening before the child enters junior high or middle school. Or it might be planned for the evening before the child promotes into the student ministry of the church. The family might discuss which of these dates seems to be the most powerful life transition.

Coordinate Family Plans with Church Plans

Parents of children approaching adolescence should ask church leaders about any church plans that might impact family plans. For example, if the church is planning an important event or celebration to welcome students into the youth group, parents might decide to plan their bar mitzvah for the night before.

Consider Christian Students with Lost Parents

Christian families can provide a ceremony for Christian students whose lost parents will not provide such an occasion. Elements should be added to the ceremony that affirm the significance of the child's actual parents and call for obedience and honor to them.

Preparation

In preparation for this special time:

1. Consider purchasing, making, or securing a lasting symbol of the event to present to the young person. For example, I purchased a real sword to present to my son. I used the sword as part of the charge that I gave him during the ceremony. The sword now is displayed in a place of honor in his bedroom and may well become a valued heirloom passed to his children some day.

2. Make a decision about how parents will participate. In homes with a Christian father, the father should take the lead with the ceremony. Single mothers should take the lead in their homes and should take all the assignments in the ceremony directed to parents. In homes with a father who is not a Christian, parents need to discuss in private what his role will be. Some non-Christian fathers may feel comfortable reading some or all of the assignments in the ceremony for fathers. Others may want to attend but have their wives do all the speaking. Still others may not want to be present for the ceremony. Though this will be a cause for sadness, Christian mothers should move forward with providing a memorable ceremony for the teenager. In the days that follow, the mother may want to invite Christian men to provide spiritual leadership for her children.

3. Make a decision about younger siblings. Some families may feel younger siblings will find the ceremony moving and will even begin looking forward to their turn. Other families may sense that younger children will want attention during the evening, will detract from the seriousness of the occasion, and will cause resentment from the teenager.

4. Straighten the house. Similar to Jewish preparations for Passover, straightening the house communicates something important is about to happen.

5. Prepare a nicer meal and use the good dishes. Again such preparations let everyone know that something important is about to happen. Candlelight for both the meal and the ceremony to follow adds richness.

6. Linger at the table. There is no need to rush the evening. The ceremony itself won't last long, so savor the moment. Consider serving the meal in relaxed courses with lots of laughter and family memories mixed in.

7. Dress the way the family dresses for Sunday morning. Keep in mind you are making memories that will last a lifetime. Preparations are worth the momentary hassle.

8. Take nicer photos. The evening likely will be one of the most special times your family will share. Parents will treasure photo memories.

9. Turn off every kind of phone. This is one of those rare moments that must be protected from any kind of interruption.

10. Plan how to sit during the ceremony. Sitting too far apart makes the ceremony seem cold. Sitting scrunched together may be too intense for some teens. Plan ahead of time where to sit and place candles and other items accordingly.

THE CEREMONY

Jewish families have the advantage of many centuries of tradition in the conducting of bar and bat mitzvahs. In reality there is no official Christian equivalent. Each family must find its own way in planning one. Here is a cafeteria of ideas families can consider.

Ceremony Possibilities

1. Court of Honor—Invite several key adults chosen by the youth, usually of the same sex as the youth. Each adult presents a charge and gives a blessing and then presents a symbol or remembrance gift of that blessing.

2. The Blessings of the Father—Kingdom parents bless the best in their children. The blessing the Jewish father gives his child during an actual bar mitzvah is powerful and life-shaping. Give careful thought to the words you will use as you bless and encourage your son or daughter. You may want to deliver the blessing while holding both of your child's hands and looking into his or her eyes.

3. The Blessings of the Mother—This blessing also is important for the present and for a lifetime. It deserves careful preparation and delivery.

4. The Charge of Names

The Charge of the Family Name—Review the meaning of the family name through research at the library or online. Present to the child the positive traits and traditions of the family name. If appropriate, present some symbol of the family name, such as a crest. Review those in previous generations or the present extended family who have been people of honor. Challenge the child to bring new honor to the family name.

The Charge of the Child's Name—Review the meaning of the child's given name through research at the library or online. If no formal meaning is available, develop a meaning for the ceremony. Present during the ceremony the meaning of the name and challenge him or her to bring honor to that name.

The Charge of the Name of Christ—Read out loud Philippians 2:5–11. Present the meaning of that name and present a charge to bring honor rather than dishonor to that name.

5. Challenge to Nobility—The kingdom person has a vital relationship to the King. Explain that Christians are on earth in part to develop the characteristics of nobility so they will be ready to rule with the King for eternity. Challenge your son or daughter to invest the next few years in those things that are noble in character. Consider presenting a sword to your son or a tiara to your daughter as a symbol of this quest for biblical nobility.

6. The Altar of Isaac—Borrow a six-foot table from the church and cover it with a sheet. Ask your son or daughter to lie on the table with arms folded. Both parents stand near the table.

Mother: We do not own you. You are the Lord's. We will not hold you so tightly that you miss God's plans and purposes for you. We will seek in every way to protect you, unless that ever becomes contrary to God's call on your life. If his clear call should involve sacrifice or risk, we will not stand in the way but will cheer you on.

Father: We will surrender our will for you to God's divine will, regardless of the cost or inconvenience to us. We will cast a vision before you of God's special plan for his glory and his plan to reach the nations of the world. We will teach you basic biblical doctrines, stewardship, and service. We will pray each day for your impact on culture and the world for God's glory.[2]

Present to your child a signed copy of what mother and father have just said.

THE TRUE LOVE WAITS HOME CEREMONY

SEVERAL MILLION CHRISTIAN TEENAGERS have made a formal promise of lifetime purity and sexual abstinence until marriage. They have found strength in this promise by linking arms with all those worldwide who have made this True Love Waits promise. The strongest True Love Waits promises are those promises teenagers make in the presence of family.

Let Your Teenager Say When He or She Is Ready

Parents frightened by the possibility of teenage immorality may try to push a teenager toward a premature promise. However, a promise that is coerced has no power to shape behavior.

Parents should teach about sexuality and about righteousness "when you walk along the road" (just in the course of family life) and "when you sit in your house" (in more formal family teaching times) (Deut. 6:7). Ideally, this should begin at the birth of a child and continue into adolescence. When the child reaches puberty, parents can explain the significance of a True Love Waits promise and ceremony.

Then from time to time, parents can say, "When you are ready to make this beautiful promise to God and celebrate it with a ceremony in our home, just let us know."

Coordinate Family Plans with Church Plans

When children reach puberty, parents need to talk with church leaders about plans for celebrating True Love Waits promises. If the church is planning a True Love Waits ceremony in the near future, then parents can customize a home experience that will complement but not duplicate what will happen at church. If church leaders have no plans for a ceremony in the near future, then parents should proceed with plans for a full ceremony at home. Once a child has developed sexually and is ready to make a formal promise to God, most parents will not want to wait years for that promise to be affirmed and celebrated.

Consider Christian Students with Lost Parents

Christian families can provide a True Love Waits ceremony for Christian students whose lost parents will not provide such an occasion. Elements should be added to the ceremony that affirm the significance of the child's actual parents and call for obedience and honor to them.

Consider the Approach with a Child
Who Is Sexually Experienced

Families aware a teenager is sexually experienced should adapt the plans below to that situation. The most important issue is ensuring the teenager now has a personal relationship with Jesus Christ. The second most important issue is ensuring the converted teenager understands repentance and grace and has experienced the reality of grace. The third most important issue is ensuring the teenager experiences grace and forgiveness from parents as well as a challenge to purity and holiness for the future. Parents might say during the ceremony, "We serve a God of second chances." Parents also can note that the True Love Waits promise is a promise "from this day" forward.

Preparation

In preparation for this very special time:

1. Order a ring or other symbol of the True Love Waits promise. True Love Waits rings or other wearable symbols are powerful reminders of the promise made. Thousands of couples being married these days have been wearing such symbols for years. In fact, many are making the exchanging of True Love Waits rings a beautiful part of their wedding vows. (For a full selection of True Love Waits rings and other wearable symbols, go to www.truelove-waits.com and click on Cool Things.) Ken Hemphill's family used beautiful gold keys with each of their girls as that symbol of purity.

2. Make a decision about how parents will participate. In homes with a Christian father, the father should take the lead with the ceremony. In homes with a single mom, she should take the lead and should take all the assignments in the ceremony directed to parents. In homes with a father who is not a Christian, parents need to discuss in private what his role will be. Some non-Christian fathers may feel comfortable reading some or all of the assignments in the ceremony for fathers. Others may want to attend but have their wives do all the speaking. Still others may not want to be present for the ceremony. Though this will be a cause for sadness, Christian mothers should move forward with providing a memorable ceremony for the teenager.

3. Make a decision about younger siblings. Some families may feel younger siblings will find the ceremony moving and will even begin looking forward to their turn. Other families may sense that younger children will want attention during the evening, will detract from the seriousness of the occasion, and will cause resentment from the teenager.

4. Straighten the house. Similar to Jewish preparations for Passover, straightening the house communicates something important is about to happen.

5. Prepare a nice meal and use the good dishes. Again such preparations let everyone know that something important is about to happen. Candlelight for both the meal and the ceremony to follow adds richness.

6. Linger at the table. There is no need to rush the evening. The ceremony itself won't last long, so savor the moment. Consider serving the meal in relaxed courses, with lots of laughter and family memories mixed in.

7. Dress the way the family dresses for Sunday morning. Keep in mind you are making memories that will last a lifetime. Preparations are worth the momentary hassle.

8. Take photos. The evening likely will be one of the most special times your family will share. Parents will treasure photo memories. A photo on display in a teenager's room also becomes another gentle reminder that the True Love Waits promise is a promise to family as well as to God.

9. Turn off every kind of phone. This is one of those rare moments that must be protected from any kind of interruption.

10. Plan how to sit during the ceremony. Sitting too far apart makes the ceremony seem cold. Sitting scrunched together may be too intense for some teens. Plan ahead of time where to sit and place candles and other items accordingly.

THE CEREMONY

Prayer—When the family is seated, the father should begin the ceremony with prayer.

Memories—Mother then should tell stories about their first moments with the child at the center of the ceremony. For some families these will be memories from the delivery room. For others it will be a precious moment in the adoption process. For still others it will be that moment of introduction when families were about to blend.

Scripture—Father should read Joshua 24:15. If appropriate, dad can give a brief testimony about his joy that the entire family is standing together for purity and righteousness.

Father's Blessing—Father should walk over to the teenager, ask the teenager to stand, and then take both of the teenager's hands. The father should give his child a blessing by expressing his love to the teenager and then naming qualities and characteristics in that child for which he is thankful. A warm hug should follow.

Mother's Blessing—Mother then should do the very same thing, using her words to express love and gratitude.

Scripture—The teenager should now lie on the floor with arms folded as if lying on an altar. (A pillow and blanket might be provided.) Then the father should stand over the teenager and read Romans 12:1. Mother should explain that moral purity is central to making our bodies living sacrifices.

Responsive Reading—When the teenager is seated again, the family should begin the responsive reading. Copies for each family member will be helpful.

Responsive Reading

Father: There was a time when many walked habitually in the pathway of the world. We lived according to the flesh, but God made us alive through Christ.

All: We commit to living as a kingdom family and to a lifetime of purity.

Father: God is rich in his mercy toward us, that while we were dead in our sins, through the grace of Jesus, we have been made alive forevermore.

All: Forgive us for the days and years we have spent watching, reading, listening, and experiencing vile and impure things.

Mother: We are each new creations today.

All: Create in each of us a clean heart, oh God. Restore your glory.

Mother: Make the crooked passages in our lives straight today.

Teenager: Restore our joy.

All: We are your children.

Parents: We will place no corrupt thing before our eyes.

Teenager: As students.

Parents: As parents.

Father: Hear, oh Lord, in this sacred hour, on this holy ground, our commitment to you and to one another.

Mother: Lord, be glorified as our child commits. (The teenager should put down his or her copy of the responsive reading at this point.)

Father: Repeat after me. Believing that true love waits . . . I make a commitment to God . . . myself . . . my family . . . my friends . . . my future mate . . . and my future children . . . to a lifetime of purity . . . including sexual abstinence . . . from this day . . . until the day I enter . . . a biblical marriage relationship. . . . (The teenager will need to pick up a copy of the responsive reading at this point while parents put their copy down.)

Teenager: Lord, be glorified as my parents commit. Repeat after me. Believing that true love is pure . . . I join my teenager . . . in committing to a lifestyle of purity. . . . I make a commitment to God . . . myself . . . my family . . . and my community of faith . . . to abstain from pornography, . . . impure touching and conversations,

. . . and sex outside a biblical marriage relationship . . . from this day forward. . . .

(Parents place the True Love Waits ring or other symbol on their teenager. The teenager and parents sign the True Love Waits promise card. Hugs and words of affection are in order.)

Mother: May this ring be a reminder of your commitment to purity. It was given you by parents who love you and support you in this commitment. Wear it with the knowledge that your purity is for God's glory. On your wedding night you are to give this ring to your spouse as a celebration of promises given and promises kept. We join you in praying that the spouse God has selected for you will make and keep the same promise for you.[1]

Prayer: Father and mother should walk behind the teenager's chair and then place their hands on their child. They should close the ceremony with prayers of love and gratitude.

CHANGING
ADULT HABITS

ADULT CHANGE IS HARD. Turning the insights from this book into permanent ways of living will not be easy. The following activity can help. For one week check off your progress on the grid below.

Give yourself a checkmark each time you:

1. Give your child a warm touch.

2. Point out to your child a strength or a positive attribute he or she has.

3. Go an entire day without using a sarcastic tone of voice with a child.

4. Listen with interest and eye contact to something your child wants to tell you.

5. Participate in an activity your child enjoys.

6. Pray with your child at bedtime.

7. Go an entire day without using the withdrawal of your warmth as a discipline technique.

8. Speak of the things of God informally or during a devotional.

9. Say, "I love you" to your child.

10. Show progress on a parenting issue you want to work on.

	M	T	W	Th	F	S
Warm touch						
Point out a strength						
No sarcasm						
Listen with interest						
An activity he/she enjoys						
Pray at bedtime						
Love not withdrawn						
Speak about God						
Say, "I love you."						
Issue you want to work on						

ENDNOTES

Chapter 1: Pastor, What Happened?

1. Glen Schultz, *Kingdom Education* (Nashville: LifeWay Press, 2002), 98.

Chapter 4: Who Children and Teenagers Think God Is

1. Christian Smith with Melinda Lundquist Denton, *Soul Searching: The Religious and Spiritual Lives of American Teenagers* (New York: Oxford University Press, 2005), 41.

2. Ibid.

3. "Current Trends at a Glance," *Youthviews* 8, no. 1, March 2001, www.gtbe.org/publications/trendwatch/tw_sep-o1_p1_graph.pdf (8 September 2004).

4. Smith and Denton, *Soul Searching*, 39.

5. Ibid., 47.

6. Ibid., 40.

7. Ibid., 65.

8. Ibid., 32.

9. Ibid., 122.

10. Ibid., 42.

11. Ibid., 44.

12. Ibid., 34.

13. Ibid., 143–45.

14. Ibid., 147.

15. Ibid., 144.

16. Ibid., 124.

17. Ibid., 130.

Chapter 5: Introducing Children and Teenagers to God

1. Smith and Denton, *Soul Searching*, 136–37.

2. Ibid., 167.

3. Ibid., 137.

4. Ibid., 136.

5. George Barna, *Real Teens* (Ventura, Calif.: Regal, 2001), 126.

6. Ibid.

7. Richard R. Dunn, *Shaping the Spiritual Life of Students* (Downers Grove, Ill.: InterVarsity Press, 2001), 59.

8. Ken Hemphill, *Empowering Kingdom Growth: The Heartbeat of God* (Nashville, Tenn.: Broadman & Holman Publishers, 2004), 303–4.

9. Tim Kimmel, *Grace Based Parenting* (Nashville: W Publishing, 2004), 35.

Chapter 6: The Adults Children and Teenagers Need

1. Smith and Denton, *Soul Searching*, 60.

2. "Survey: High Schoolers Appreciate Family Times," *Associated Press* (Washington), 6 August 2003, 1.

3. Ibid.

4. Gary Chapman, *The Five Love Languages of Teenagers* (Chicago: Northfield Publishing: 2000), 33, quoting Lawrence Steinberg.

5. David J. Welsh, "The Canaries of Our Society," *Fort Worth Star-Telegram*, June 2004.

6. Smith and Denton, *Soul Searching*, 120.

7. Ibid., 56.

8. Chapman, *The Five Love Languages of Teenagers*, 12.

9. Merton P. Strommen and Richard A. Hardel, *Passing On the Faith: A Radical New Model for Youth and Family Ministry* (Minnesota: Saint Mary's Press, 2000), 85.

10. Bruce Wilkinson, *The Three Chairs: Experiencing Spiritual Breakthroughs* (Nashville: LifeWay Press, 1999), 12–13.

11. T. W. Hunt, *The Mind of Christ: The Transforming Power of Thinking His Thoughts* (Nashville, Tenn.: Broadman & Holman Publishers, 1995), 160–61.

12. Henry Blackaby, "Guiding the Family in Times of Uncertainty" *Baptist Press*, 6 July 2004.

13. David Hutchins, *Courageous Parenting: The Passionate Pursuit of Your Teen's Heart* (Colorado: Navpress, 2000), 8–9.

14. Ibid., 10.

15. N. Lezin, L. Rolleri, S. Bean, & J. Taylor, *Parent-Child Connectedness: Implication for Research, Interventions and Positive Impacts on Adolescent Health* (Santa Cruz, Calif.: ETR Associates, 2004), viii.

16. Bruce H. Wilkinson, *30 Days to Experiencing Spiritual Breakthroughs* (Sisters, Ore.: Multnomah Publishers, 1999), 244–45.

17. Lezin, et. al., *Parent-Child Connectedness*, 40.

18. Ibid., viii.

19. Josh McDowell, "It's Almost Too Late," *New Man Magazine*, June 2003, 56.

20. Hutchins, *Courageous Parenting*, 23.

21. Strommen and Hardel, *Passing On the Faith*, 32.

22. Ibid., 63.

23. Wilkinson, *Experiencing Spiritual Breakthroughs*, 224–25.

24. Hutchins, *Courageous Parenting*, 36.

25. Scott Larson and Larry Brendtro, *Reclaiming Our Prodigal Sons and Daughters: A Practical Approach for Connecting with Youth in Conflict* (Bloomington, Ind.: National Educational Service, 1999), 106.

26. Chapman, *The Five Love Languages of Teenagers*, 249–50.

27. Hutchins, *Courageous Parenting*, 36.

28. Karen Dockrey, *Bold Parents, Positive Teens* (Colorado: WaterBrook Press, 2002), 7.

29. Wilkinson, *Experiencing Spiritual Breakthroughs*, 247.

30. M. Eisenberg, *Archives of Pediatrics and Adolescent Medicine*, vol. 158 (August 2004): 792–96.

31. Wilkinson, *Experiencing Spiritual Breakthroughs*, 216–17.

32. Reb Bradley, *Beyond Obedience: Raising Children Who Love God and Others*, adapted from chapter 15 of *Child Training Tips*, expanded edition, http://www.familyministries.com.

33. Dockrey, *Bold Parents, Positive Teens*, 22.

34. Bradley, *Beyond Obedience*, http://www.familyministries.com.

35. Jim Burns, "Parenting with A.W.E." *Christianity Today International/Christian Parenting Today Magazine*, Spring 2004, 24.

36. Hutchins, *Courageous Parenting*, 66.

37. Chapman, *The Five Love Languages of Teenagers*, 34.

38. Ken McAlpine, "The Young and the Restless," *American Way Magazine*, 1 December 2003, 42.

39. Cindy Krishcer Goodman, "Giving Up Second Income May Be No Sacrifice," *Knight Ridder News Service*, 13 April 2003.

40. Strommen and Hardel, *Passing On the Faith*, 38.

41. Bradley, *Beyond Obedience*, http://www.familyministries.com. All four of these bullet points are quoted from this source.

42. Kathleen Kline, *Hardwired to Connect: The New Scientific Case for Authoritative Communities* (New York: Institute for American Values, 2003), 27.

43. Smith and Denton, *Soul Searching*, 275–76.

44. Kline, *Hardwired to Connect*, 37.

45. Strommen and Hardel, *Passing On the Faith*, 176.

46. Mark Matlock, *Generation Hope: Preparing Today's Young People for a Lifetime of Purpose* (Friendswood, Tex.: Baxter Press, 2002), 59.

47. Smith and Denton, *Soul Searching*, 269.

Chapter 7: Impacting Children and Teenagers at Home

1. Ben Freudenburg and Rick Lawrence, *The Family-Friendly Church* (Loveland, Colo.: Group Publishing, 1998), 10.

2. Josh McDowell, "It's Almost Too Late," *New Man Magazine*, June 2003, 56.

3. Scott Larson and Larry Brendtro, *Reclaiming Our Prodigal Sons and Daughters: A Practical Approach for Connecting with Youth in Conflict* (Bloomington, Ind.: National Educational Service, 1999), 99.

4. Strommen and Hardel, *Passing On the Faith*, 14.

5. Ibid.

6. Ibid., 98.

7. Wilkinson, *Experiencing Spiritual Breakthroughs*, 212.

8. Strommen and Hardel, *Passing On the Faith*, 88–93.

9. Ibid.

10. Ibid.

11. Henry Blackaby, "Guiding the Family in Times of Uncertainty," *Baptist Press* (Atlanta, Ga.: 6 July 2004).

12. Glen Schultz, *Kingdom Education* (Nashville: LifeWay Press, 2002), 38.

13. Ibid., 46.

14. Smith and Denton, *Soul Searching*, 269.

15. Tom Elliff and Robert Witty, *In Their Own Words* (Nashville: Broadman & Holman, 2003).

16. Mark Matlock, *Generation Hope: Preparing Today's Young People for a Lifetime of Purpose* (Texas: Baxter Press, 2002), 23.

17. Wilkinson, *Experiencing Spiritual Breakthroughs*, 269.

18. James Dobson, *The New Dare to Discipline* (Wheaton, Ill.: Tyndale House Publishers, 1992), 51.

19. Lezin, Rolleri, et. al., *Parent-Child Connectedness*, 9.

20. Strommen and Hardel, *Passing On the Faith*, 179.

21. Gary Smalley, *Love Is a Decision* (Dallas: Word Publishing, 1989), 171.

Chapter 8: Impacting Children and Teenagers at Church

1. Smith and Denton, *Soul Searching*, 161.

2. Ibid.

3. Ibid.

4. Strommen and Hardel, *Passing On the Faith*, 14.

5. Smith and Denton, *Soul Searching*, 263.

6. Mark Regnerus, Christian Smith, and Melissa Fritsch, "Religion in the Lives of American Adolescents: A Review of the Literature," *National Study of Youth and Religion*, no. 3 (2003): 20.

7. Ibid., 29.

8. Ibid., 32.

9. Ibid., 7.

10. Kline, *Hardwired to Connect*, 30.

11. Ibid., 31.

12. Chris Smith, "Theorizing Religious Effects Among American Adolescents," *Journal for the Scientific Study of Religion* 42:1 (2003): 17–30.

13. Smith and Denton, *Soul Searching*, 124.

14. Ibid., 266.

15. Ibid., 267.

16. Ibid., 148.

17. Matlock, *Generation Hope*, 30.

18. Smith and Denton, *Soul Searching*, 267.

Chapter 9: Releasing Children and Teenagers to the Kingdom

1. Mark Matlock, *Generation Hope: Preparing Today's Young People for a Lifetime of Purpose* (Texas: Baxter Press, 2002), 16.

2. Robert Jamieson, A. R. Fausset, and David Brown, *Commentary Critical and Explanatory on the Whole Bible* (1871).

3. John Piper, from an unpublished sermon at the OneDay gathering of collegians (Sherman, Tex.: 16 May 2003).

The Christian Bar/Bat Mitzvah at Home

1. J. Otis Ledbetter and Tim Smith, *Family Traditions* (Colorado Springs: Focus on the Family, 2000).

2. Adapted from Mark Matlock, *Generation Hope*.

The True Love Waits Home Ceremony

1. Adapted from *True Love Waits: Goes Home* (Nashville: LifeWay Press, 2002), 47.